A SHORT GUIDE TO ETHICAL RISK

SHORT GUIDES TO RISK SERIES

Risk is a far more complex and demanding issue than it was ten years ago. Risk managers may have expertise in the general aspects of risk management and in the specifics that relate directly to their business, but they are much less likely to understand other more specialist risks. Equally, Company Directors may find themselves falling down in their duty to manage risk because they don't have enough knowledge to be able to talk to their risk team in a sensible way.

The short guides to risk are not going to make either of these groups experts in the subject but will give them plenty to get started and in a format and an extent (circa 100 pages) that is readily digested.

Titles in the series will include:

- Climate Risk
- Compliance Risk
- Employee Risk
- Environmental Risk
- Fraud Risk
- Information Risk
- Intellectual Property Risk
- Kidnap and Ransom Risk
- Operational Risk
- Purchasing Risk
- Reputation Risk
- Strategic Risk
- Supply Chain Risk
- Tax Risk
- Terrorism Risk

For further information, visit www.gowerpublishing.com/shortguidestorisk.

A Short Guide to Ethical Risk

Carlo Patetta Rotta

Translation by Paolo Cortucci and Inderjeet Gill

GOWER

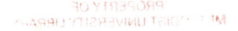

Published by
Gower Publishing Limited
Wey Court East
Union Road
Farnham
Surrey GU9 7PT
England
www.gowerpublishing.com

Gower Publishing Company
Suite 420
101 Cherry Street
Burlington, VT 05401-4405
USA

174.4
R85I5
2010

British Library Cataloguing in Publication Data
Rotta, Carlo Patetta.
   A short guide to ethical risk.
   1. Business ethics. 2. Social responsibility of business.
   3. Corporations--Corrupt practices--Prevention.
   I. Title
   658.4'08-dc22

   ISBN: 978-0-566-09172-8 (pbk)
   ISBN: 978-0-566-09173-5 (ebk)

Library of Congress Cataloging-in-Publication Data
Rotta, Carlo Patetta.
   A short guide to ethical risk / by Carlo Patetta Rotta.
     p. cm. -- (Short guides to business risk)
   Includes bibliographical references and index.
   ISBN 978-0-566-09172-8 (hbk) -- ISBN 978-0-566-09173-5
   (ebook) 1. Business ethics. 2. Social responsibility of business. 3. Economics-
   -Moral and ethical aspects. I. Title.
   HF5387.R676 2010
   174'.4--dc22

                                                        2009050641

Mixed Sources
Product group from well-managed
forests and other controlled sources
www.fsc.org Cert no. SA-COC-1565
© 1996 Forest Stewardship Council
FSC

Printed and bound in Great Britain by
MPG Books Group, UK

Contents

12·27·2011 Amazon $34.95

Acknowledgements

My sincerest thanks to those friends and colleagues who have supported me in my desire to research and write about ethics in business, and who did not consider me just an incurable "romantic" even before the financial crisis of 2008. In particular, I would like to thank Alessandra Riorda, Anastasia Liapi, Paola Baravalle, Laura Scaramella, Claudio Chiaves, John Purkiss and Nancy Haig.

My most heartfelt thanks to those professionals who have done their utmost to revise and support my research and writing. In particular, I wish to acknowledge:

- Melissa Whitman and John Small, Fraud Investigation & Dispute Services department of the London office of Ernst & Young.

- Rosalind Wright, Chairman of the UK Fraud Advisory Panel.

- Prof. Geoffrey Hodgson, Professor of Business Studies at the University of Hertfordshire, UK.

- Prof. Gilberto Muraro, Professor of "Scienza delle Finanze" at University of Padua, Italy.

- Vincenzo Tessandori, reporter for the Italian newspaper *La Stampa* and book author.

- Roy Snell, Chief Executive Officer, Society of Corporate Compliance and Ethics.

A special thank you to my father who liked the idea of me writing this book and who always supported me in achieving this objective.

Foreword

"...he that filches from me my good name
Robs me of that which not enriches him
And makes me poor indeed."

Othello, Act 3 Scene 3

Until comparatively recently, few company directors, let alone risk managers would have considered the ethical dimension of a business decision as having any meaningful impact on the success or otherwise of the business itself. To succeed, it was vital to act decisively, even ruthlessly, to compete at all costs with the opposition, even if that meant cutting ancillary costs such as wages and staff training to the bone and ignoring any factors not directly relevant to the "bottom line". It has taken a deep worldwide recession to force business leaders to focus their minds on wider considerations in determining what makes a successful business.

Those directing minds on boards who have long known the value of a reputation founded securely on good ethical principles – integrity, dealing honestly with employees, suppliers and customers, having respect for the environment and assuming corporate and social responsibility – have shown that even when economic times are hard, their businesses succeed and come through. Businesses which nurture their staff, institute proper training programmes and instil an ethical culture, leading "from the top", with senior managers and directors leading by example, are observing the right values for business and are counted amongst the most successful in their field. Employees who feel confident that their concerns are heeded and that they can "speak up" without fear of victimisation will be loyal to their company and feel they have a real share in its product.

On the other hand, businesses whose bosses are known to behave corruptly or dishonestly, ignore staff concerns, deal inadequately with complaints from customers or suppliers, will feel the adverse impact, reflected in poor production, rapid staff turnover and disloyal and dishonest staff, who will be prepared to betray the business and its customers. This behaviour, which is damaging in itself to the economic health of the company, will become doubly dangerous if it develops into full-scale fraud.

I am in the "fraud" business. I have spent over 25 years pursuing and prosecuting criminals who have committed crimes of deception and dishonesty and been caught. Many of those who have come across my desk have been directors of businesses, most of which have failed, sometimes as a direct result of the criminality alleged. A fine line divides the unethical from the frankly dishonest and fraudulent. What starts, often, as corner-cutting, or short-term borrowing from the company – which is well illustrated in this book in "The Fraud Triangle Theory", described on p. 49, the well-known triplet "pressure, opportunity and rationalisation", becomes an irresistible way of life for some, and eventually turns into full-blown fraud. What is of concern to us all are the many who have adopted this pattern of behaviour and haven't yet been caught; they could be working in your firm.

Senior management and the risk manager in today's company cannot afford to be complacent about the risk of fraud. Prevention of fraud starts with instilling an ethical culture in the business. Ethics are not an optional add-on, something "nice" to have and touchy-feely which can be featured as a side-note in the company's Annual Report. Good business practice and ethical behaviour are intrinsic to a successful business and are the best defence against fraud. Every company should have an ethical policy statement, which is published to every employee of the company and is simple enough to be self-explanatory. It should start at the bottom, with the most basic requirements, applied to every level of the organisation, setting the limits of what the company itself considers to be acceptable behaviour – whether it is the acceptance of corporate hospitality, making private phone calls on the office phone or taking home items of office stationery. On an overall basis, the policy statement should explain to its employees that all the company's practices must reflect honesty, integrity and concern for others; that each person employed by the company at every level is responsible for all his or her actions and decisions; and that the company and all its staff comply with the letter, spirit and intention of the laws, rules and regulations that apply to it.

A company that lives by these principles will have a secure basis to guard against the risk of fraud and enhance its reputation in the market place. It is the risk manager's job to ensure that these sound principles are carried into practice.

Carlo Patetta Rotta's excellent book, which I am delighted to introduce, is a practical guide as to how the risk manager and senior management which must support him in his vital role, can put this into practice in the day-to-day management of the company's business.

Rosalind Wright CB QC
Chairman, Fraud Advisory Panel, UK

Preface

I have always been attracted by the complex analysis of moral dilemmas that we have to face as individuals and members of structured organisations, such as civil society or the companies where we work. This attitude comes from the awareness of the numerous consequences of our decisions that have repercussions not just on ourselves but on others too.

As I have been working for a number of years as an internal auditor for large corporations and have, therefore, been responsible for ensuring ethics within my companies, I have a professional as well as a general interest in ethics. When in 2009, Gower decided to publish a series of short guides on specific risks, they proposed that I deal with the guide on the "ethical" risk, particularly topical following the financial crisis that is ongoing at the time of writing.

Joining this initiative was something of a challenge because I thought that it was difficult to deal with such an abstract and subjective theme such as ethics applied to business in the shape of a guide, that is to say with content that is ready to be applied with almost scientific rigour. Nonetheless, I was fully aware – in the light of recent events in the global economy too – of the usefulness of adopting a more practical approach to structure a complex subject that, over the centuries, has been widely debated by philosophers and economists. Following this consideration, I decided to undertake the challenging task of writing this book.

I hope that readers will gain better understanding of the main issues and most recent developments of this subject and, in particular, that those who work in the field of corporate ethics can identify some useful advice to apply within their organisations.

"The first step in the evolution of ethics is a sense of solidarity with other human beings."

Albert Schweitzer 1875–1965, German missionary doctor and theologian, winner of the Nobel Peace prize

"It's not hard to make decisions when you know what your values are."

Roy Disney, American scriptwriter and producer, nephew of Walt Disney

"The world is a dangerous place, not because of those who do evil, but because of those who look on and do nothing."

Albert Einstein

Introduction

In today's world, ethics in business, in the practical sense of following fundamental moral principles in transactions of an economic nature, no longer seems to be in line with public expectations. For an economic system as a whole to work in a balanced fashion, the ethics being adhered to must, among other things, be in line with what the conscience of each individual perceives to be "good" and "right". This point, though seemingly trivial, needs careful reflection.

In the wake of the financial scandals of the beginning of the millennium, including those of Enron and Parmalat, and with the onset in summer 2008 of an international financial crisis set off by the US sub-prime mortgages, the debate on the ethical aspect of business has greatly intensified and has become richer. Public opinion can be said to agree on the fact that the current ethical "level" in the business world is unacceptable. Consequently, both a practical and theoretical search for appropriate solutions to revert this trend is being urged. While it may be true that this is a complex, uneasy and age-old issue, it does not mean that it can be left in the exclusive control of the "invisible Smithsonian hand", i.e., those dynamics that are intrinsic to the free market. On the contrary! An in-depth and pragmatic discussion is needed in an attempt to create a culture that revolves more around ethics and to identify a series of tools that can be of assistance in reaching this objective.

As in every field, in the context of business ethics is a constantly evolving discipline. For its own intrinsic nature, ethics cannot be understood without considering factors such as the historic-cultural context, religious sensitivity, and the political and social climate. The development of modern democracies, for instance, has led to the widespread adoption of rights in the economic sectors that are recognised for everyone – like the right to remuneration proportionate to the quality and quantity of work, the right to a weekly rest and parity between the sexes – which, in the past, had not always been given the same attention as they receive today. However, conduct that for a long time was considered irrelevant to the sphere of morality, or that was merely tolerated in that sphere, is today considered immoral and is disapproved of, if not sanctioned. Just think of mobbing at the workplace that is a constant, aggressive and unmotivated behaviour adopted by a boss/manager towards a subordinate and aimed at psychologically humiliating the latter. Another such behaviour is sexual harassment, i.e., continuous and unsolicited advances in the workplace. Even though national legal systems do not always define these behaviours as crimes, they do, however, tend to prosecute them more often than in the past. Companies' codes of conduct tend to include these behaviours among those that employees have to refrain from adopting.

In my capacity as an auditor of multinationals, I am always committed to finding the most appropriate answers to such questions as:

- What duty do companies owe towards the environment in which they operate or the communities from which they hire their labour?

- When does advertising a product turn into an instrument of manipulation?

- When does discerning tax planning become evasion?

- Where may the line be drawn between fair and unfair competition? Is complying with the rules of the anti-trust watchdog sufficient?

- What constitutes an acceptable financial statements strategy and when does it become a false public statement misrepresenting the assets as well as the financial and economic situation of a company?

- How can a conflict of interest arising in a company be defined? And where is the boundary between cases which are acceptable and those which should be avoided?

Although I have posed these questions from an auditor's point of view, by widening the context it is clear that similar questions are well known to anyone in the business world trying to work with propriety and responsibility. It is also clear that the questions I have posed above – or similar questions – cannot be answered without reference to some ethical framework and consequently each individual's response could, at least in part, vary, as it will inevitably reflect his personal "history" and values. In fact, in the economic field, not unlike other fields where ethics applies, it is unrealistic to expect to identify right or wrong answers *per se*. It is more appropriate to verify each time their soundness as a function of the strength and coherence of the reasoning that precipitates the action or decision being morally judged.

Therefore, expressing a judgement on the ethical nature of a decision is a delicate task, since analysis should not limit itself to considering solely the fact in itself, but also the factors that may have caused it. It is also important to understand how each individual factor has affected the decision. This approach is similar to that of a judge who, when studying documents relating to a case, must hear witnesses and analyse any evidence submitted before pronouncing his verdict. Clearly, this process is neither immediate nor smooth. In addition, the undeniable difficulty in carrying out an assessment objectively must not be used as an alibi to shelve the problem or to state *a priori* that it cannot be solved. To do so would be akin to a judge who thinks that it is too uncomfortable to perform an in-depth examination of the background of a case, and who therefore decides not to carry out the necessary investigations and so gives up on finding the truth and administering justice; or, even worse, decides to pass a summary and shallow judgement. Some might object and argue that, whereas there is a strong subjective element within the field of ethics, the legal and judicial system is founded on accurate laws contained in specific codes. This is quite true. However, as outlined in this study, many national and international guidelines have been issued over the last few years and it is now common practice, at least as far as large companies are concerned, to adopt codes of ethics and internal procedures to ensure that all employees share these guidelines, and to monitor compliance with basic ethical principles when they are not part of the identity of the organisation itself. If it is true that much has to be done to have more ethics within companies – and this book wants to provide practical help in this sense – the fact that much has already been done over the last few years at international level has to be borne in mind.

At economic and legal level, some of the areas where significant progress has been made are:

- More specific and coercive regulations;

- New models of governance, that is to say hierarchical relationships between the various company roles, aimed at ensuring greater transparency and clearer responsibilities;

- The creation of associations providing specific support to practitioners in charge of ethics within companies (see list of associations in Chapter 7, Section 7.4);

- Increase in research.

At company level, some of the most important progress has been:

- The creation of new roles, such as that of the chief ethics officer;

- Increased attention to identifying risks within companies, including those that are strictly ethical in nature;

- The creation and adoption of new tools such as codes of ethics and whistle blowing procedures;

- Employee training on ethical values recognised by their companies and on ensuing problems.

The awareness of civil society and, as a consequence, that of companies, has significantly increased and it looks as if a process has been started that is bound to develop further.

① Ethics According to Economists

1.1 UTILITARIANISM AND ADAM SMITH

Greek philophers, from Aristippus to Epicurus, had already described man as a passive, hedonistic, individualistic and fundamentally selfish being. Thomas Hobbes, an English philosopher who lived in the 17th century, had supported the well-known pessimistic view of human nature, whereby *homo homini lupus* (man is a wolf to his fellow man).

Later, this line of thinking was supported by mercantilistic thought, as it did not have any confidence in the mind's ability to come up with sound moral or political concepts. In particular, Bernard de Mandeville, a Dutch philosopher who lived in England in late 17th century, brilliantly described in his famous satire *The Fable of the Bees: or, Private Vices, Publick Benefits* the problem of reconciling certain undesirable human characteristics, such as greed and malice, with the community's interests. Using an exaggerated representation of the economic effect of the quest for self-interest, Mandeville concluded that the welfare of a people was dependent on the efficacy of selfish motives, which were considered to be the only stimuli of individual economic behaviour. So much so that he stated that trade and honesty were incompatible, because complying with the rules set by honesty led to the downfall of the community. *"Nothing* – says Mandeville – *pushes men to be obliging if not their needs, and mitigating them is wise, but eliminating them would be foolish."*

Based on these assumptions, economic science used to adopt a neutral attitude towards any ethical logic. If economic activities by themselves aim at producing something good, we are implicitly saying that there is a sphere within social relations – pertaining to the market – that does not need to be morally judged at all. Unlike any other type of human action, economic actions have the undeniable advantage of evading morality without being against it. When pursuing their own interests, not only do individuals act properly for their own accord but they also optimise collective usefulness because the market automatically tends to settle any dispute in favour of a higher state of welfare.

In the 18th century, Adam Smith, the Scottish philosopher considered to be the father of modern economics, developed an economic theory that was to be influential in centuries to come, too. Smith supported a *laissez-faire* policy where economic forces regulate themselves on condition that they are not influenced by external policies or intervention, such as government intervention. If his theory was completely different from mercantilism, where heavy state intervention was necessary to harness economic forces, from the point of view of ethics applied to economics, his vision was, and still is, rather unclear. In fact, it looks as if his (not so loyal) epigons have summarised his impressive volume of acute reflections in a single sentence from *The Wealth of Nations* that was to become the most authoritative consecration of utilitarian theory. In 1776, Adam Smith wrote:

> *It is not from the benevolence of the butcher, the brewer, or the baker that we expect our dinner, but from their regard to their own interest. We address ourselves, not to their humanity but to their self-love, and never talk to them of our own necessities but of their advantages.*[1]

What did Adam Smith really mean to say here? Clearly, he maintains that pursuing selfish interests is sufficient to motivate and drive the exchange of goods, and we do not need to resort to ethics to explain why the baker wants to sell bread, why we want to buy it, and how this exchange would benefit both. This irrefutable statement cannot but confirm the plain observation that many of our actions are, in reality, driven by personal interest, and that some of them actually have a positive outcome. It would undoubtedly be an exaggeration to believe that Adam Smith reduced human behaviour in its entirety to servile selfishness. At any rate, over time this observation, however unquestionably true, has become instrumental in the estrangement of economics from ethics. This took place precisely and significantly at the same time as modern economics flourished. Furthermore, in comparison with alternative theories, from Smith's days up to recent years, utilitarianism has greatly influenced the way in which economic transactions are conceived and dealt with. The utilitarian concept characterises the majority of economic subjects in today's capitalist world.

---

1   Smith A., *The Wealth of Nations*, Penguin Books Ltd, 1999.

1.2 BEYOND UTILITARIANISM: AMARTYA K. SEN

In recent years, some economists and scholars have used sound arguments to openly criticise this narrow utilitarian vision, which has finally created a real opening within utilitarian absolutism for alternative theories and concepts. The most recent and significant argument has been put forward by Amartya K. Sen,[2] Nobel prize winner (1998), who fiercely and convincingly criticised a canonical interpretation of Smithsonian thinking on ethics applied to economics.

In his opinion, the fact that over time commentators and scholars have only concentrated on selected passages written by Adam Smith and neglected the remainder of his vast output, means we are shown the father of modern economic science as a rather narrow-minded ideologist whose only aim is to extol the fundamental virtues of selfish behaviour. Amartya K. Sen wrote that:

> *While some men have been living in banality ever since they were born and some find themselves living in banality after being born, Smith had the misfortune of having a lot of banality thrown at him.*[3]

Summarising Adam Smith's thinking with the terse and incisive apologia of the selfishness that was attributed to him is, therefore, restrictive. Indeed, Adam Smith spent a great deal

---

2   Amartya K. Sen's main contribution to economics is a new notion of development that is different from the previous notion of growth. Economic development no longer coincides with an increase in income but with an increase in the quality of life. It is this focus on quality, rather than quantity, that characterises most of the studies of this economist.

3   Sen, Amartya K., *La ricchezza della ragione. Denaro, valori, identità*, il Mulino, Bologna, 2001, p. 93; this is a collection of five essays published in Italian discussing ethics in business.

of his life maintaining the need for "sympathy" in behaviour that involved relating with others, and exploring the role of "moral sentiments" in building a better world. He devoted an entire book to these sentiments entitled *"The Theory of Moral Sentiments"* (1759), in which he carried out an in-depth study of the role of moral codes of behaviour – good reasons to go against the dictates of self-interest. In the book he describes and highlights the importance of feelings such as sympathy, generosity and a sense of community.

There would be no intellectual integrity in ignoring the fact that Adam Smith had assumed the existence of a fundamental system of "norms of civil and economic morality" to corroborate his argument, nor in believing that he meant that all economic operations involved simply an exchange. In relation to the first point, a more faithful interpretation of Smith's universe demonstrates that the market has a strict need to be founded on rules of honesty and trust that do not slow down transactions disastrously. If they were in force, then the market would be able to function *even* if the *ulterior* motives of the individuals who are part of it were exclusively based on self-interest.

With regard to the second point, however, it would be both reductive and unrealistic to limit the discussion on economic transactions to exchange activities without taking into due account the starting point and key process: *production*. The motivational problems around production are quite separate from those relating to exchange and are often characterised by team spirit, diligence, reliability (when there are no checks), and efficiency. Can all these fundamental attributes be ignored by hoping to summarise them as one single selfish motive? Also, would it be realistic to neglect the fact that market efficiency is deeply influenced by the degree of trust between the parties involved? If self-interest were the only concern and the only driver of behaviour, there would certainly be many opportunities where leaving the other party in an exchange by themselves would undoubtedly be sensible. However, by behaving in this way, commercial activities would be based exclusively on a recourse to the law and would, as a consequence, become extremely expensive and painfully slow. Clearly, such a view of economics would be somewhat unrealistic and deeply undesirable.

Amartya Sen writes that:

> *A business world without moral codes would not only be poor from a regulatory point of view but also very weak in terms of performance.*[4]

If one believes that economics should concern real people, then it is also worth reflecting on the fact that a partial and distorted interpretation of Smithsonian logic is not unimportant.

> *It is difficult to believe that real people can be totally uninfluenced by the magnitude of self-examination induced by the Socratic question: "How must we live?". Is it possible that people studied by economics [...] stick to the rudimentary stubborness that modern economics attributes to them?*[5]

---

4   Sen, Amartya K., *La ricchezza della ragione. Denaro, valori, identità*, il Mulino, Bologna, 2001, p. 96; this is a collection of five essays published in Italian discussing ethics in business.
5   Sen Amartya K., *On Ethics and Economics*, Oxford, Basil Blackwell, 1987, Laterza, Roma-Bari, 1988, p. 8

1.3 ETHICS FOR MODERN ECONOMISTS

Liberal thought developed in England in the 19th century following the French Revolution, and subsequently both the industrial revolution and the popularity of Adam Smith's studies. According to this school of thought, the market is a place for free enterprise, in that it prescribes the abolition of customs duties as one of its fundamental principles. State intervention in the economy is, at most, limited to building adequate infrastructure, roads and railways that can promote trade.

One of the most important supporters of liberalism was Nobel prize winner Milton Friedman, who died recently. Friedman's thinking had an extraordinary popularity and characterised international economics throughout the 20th century with extreme influence over both the American government at the time of Nixon and Reagan, and the Thatcher government in the UK. The fundamental points of the economic policies of these governments were: limited government intervention when regulating markets, control of inflation, reduction in the tax burden and strict monetary policies by central banks.

The following statements made by Milton Friedman clearly summarise his passionate and fervent vision of the need for a free market.

> *A free market gives people what they want instead of what a particular group thinks they ought to want. Underlying most arguments against the free market is a lack of belief in freedom itself. The existence of a free market does not of course eliminate the need for government. On the contrary, government is essential both as a forum for determining the "rules of the*

game" and as an umpire to interpret and enforce the rules decided on. What the market does is to reduce greatly the range of issues that must be decided through political means, and thereby to minimize the extent to which government need participate directly in the game.[6]

Milton Friedman took part in the debate on ethics in economics with "The Social Responsibility of Business is to Increase its Profits",[7] an article that caused quite a stir, particularly amongst contemporary economists. In this article, Friedman upholds a rather categorical and surprising thesis, according to which a company that fulfils its social responsibility does not behave in a morally desirable manner but commits an immoral act. When management executives, Friedman explains, decide to use company funds for a social cause, whose end is not that of maximising profits, they do not fulfil the responsibility they took on when they accepted the task of managing the company on behalf of its owners.

Over the years, long debates have been held about the responsibilities of company executives: should they be concerned only with maximising company profits or should they also consider initiatives that have a social purpose, such as supporting employees, safeguarding the environment, or assisting the community in which the company operates? The final answer to this question came from the judgement in *Dodge v Ford*[8] in the United States, which involved two families at the beginning of the 20th century who had created

---

6   *From Capitalism and Freedom* by Milton Friedman, University of Chicago Press, 1962, chapter "The Relation Between Economic Freedom and Political Freedom".

7   Milton Friedman's article in question is "The Social Responsibility of Business is to Increase its Profits", *New York Times*, 1970.

8   *The Corporation*, Joel Bakan, Constable, London 2004, p. 36.

two of the largest stars-and-stripe car companies in the world: the only responsibility management has is to always maximise company profits for the benefit of shareholders. This judgement sanctioned, once and for all, the principle of *"the best interest of the corporation"*, which is now recognised internationally and included in the Company Law of most countries.

Although Milton Friedman is a staunch enemy of corporate social responsibility, he himself specified that it has nothing to do with the notion of ethics.[9] Since the only driving force of business is the principle of profit maximisation, trying to define it on an ethical plane does not make sense because, by definition, it is not ethical. Ethics is a characteristic that can only be associated with people. In this regard, Friedman states that ethical problems might appear difficult to solve. However, in his opinion, the real difficulty is that of applying their solutions.

Friedman considers whether the manufacturing of cigarettes is immoral. His personal answer is that it is not, because today's consumers are informed about the damage caused by smoking, whether they find themselves in the position to freely decide to smoke or not. Here too, he seems to be wanting to safeguard the principle of freedom, by which he sets great store. Furthermore, he maintains that, if manufacturing cigarettes is thought to be unethical, then, similarly, cars, skis, swimming suits, etc. should not be manufactured because they are all goods linked to activities that, unless they are properly performed, can cause

---

9   From "A Question of Ethics", an article published in *Stanford Business*, a magazine of the Stanford Graduate School of Business, November 2000, Vol. 69, No. 1. The article is a transcript of a debate held by a panel of prominent figures from the economic world, Milton Friedman being one of them, who met at the Stanford Graduate School of Business during celebrations for the 75th anniversary of the School.

serious damage. If, for Friedman, manufacturing cigarettes isn't morally reprehensible, falsifying company information, on the other hand, does appear to be so.

A rather different view from Friedman's, and one that decidedly gives more weight to ethics in economics, is that of Kirk Hanson, director of the Markkula Center for Applied Ethics and Professor of Organizations and Companies at Santa Clara University in California. According to Hanson, there are three possible approaches to this problem: the first is one followed by those who deny that ethics can play a role in the world of economics; the second is that of those who believe that ethics turns those who practise it into excellent businessmen because in the long run ethics pays dividends and entails advantages; and the third is that of those who believe that ethics is an absolute value and that, therefore, it must always come before self-interest.[10]

Hanson states that he is among those who believe 90 per cent of the time that *"ethics is good business"* and for the remaining 10 per cent that it is actually moral conflict. The only approach to overcoming these is the view that sees ethics as an absolute value to be placed before any economic consideration. In discussing with Friedman the dilemma faced by cigarette manufacturers, Hanson believes that those who manufacture them are unethical. The fact that the worker in the cigarette factory has to safeguard and keep his job should not prevent him from recognising the immoral nature of this activity. In Hanson's opinion, this is the correct attitude to adopt because

---

10   From "A Question of Ethics", an article published in *Stanford Business*, a magazine of the Stanford Graduate School of Business, November 2000, Vol. 69, No. 1. The article is a transcript of a debate held by a panel of prominent figures from the economic world, Milton Friedman being one of them, who met at the Stanford Graduate School of Business during celebrations for the 75th anniversary of the School.

it is the one that, by creating social tension, has some chance of leading to changes in the long term. This behaviour, in fact, strengthens public awareness of these types of dilemmas and issues, as does pressure on politicians so that they can make changes to the legislative and regulatory systems that would take these moral requirements into consideration.

The affinity of Hanson's vision to what is happening today following the global financial crisis of 2008 is revealing. Public opinion, exasperated by the consequences of this crisis, is exerting pressure on politicians to change the regulatory and legislative systems in order to remedy the disappointing ethical level that the financial crisis has brought to light. Some countries have already introduced rules to strengthen the inspecting and sanctioning powers of supervisory bodies and have modified remuneration and incentive systems used in their banking sectors. Presumably, these are only initial reactions and the first timid attempts at undertaking a process of change that will be long-lasting and challenging considering that, to achieve the desired effects, it would have to be global.

1.4 SUSTAINABLE DEVELOPMENT AND SOCIAL RESPONSIBILITY

The fact that in the 20th century market economy imposed itself on the business world, at the same time as the economic and political liberalism was gaining ground, should lead us to think about the close link between business and civil life and, more specifically, to the relationship between the "rationality" of economic processes and the benefit they bring to society.

According to these new theories, economics becomes a tool that can be used to carry out activities that comprise a spirit of participation, solidarity, pluralism, and respect for the environment and human rights, and its objectives are in line with the cultural and civil goals that are typical of real social service. Economics becomes a useful and innovative tool in a society that is oriented more towards man and a respect for the most virtuous laws of democratic and civil life. One of the consequences of this new vision of economics is the development of the notion of Corporate Social Responsibility, or CSR. Corporate Social Responsibility is currently the centre of attention at international organisations of utmost authority, from the UN (The Global Compact) to the EU (Green Paper on Corporate Social Responsibility). The European Union, in particular, has defined this new vision of corporate responsibility as follows:

> ... companies integrate social and environmental concerns in their business operations and in their interaction with their stakeholders on a voluntary basis.[11]

In spite of the aversion to economic thought of that time, and the authoritativeness of some of his detractors, including Milton Friedman, in recent years the theory of corporate social responsibility has gained a lot of ground and is now internationally recognised and commonplace. In particular, the rationale behind corporate social responsibility was developed in the USA in the 1920s, a country where new types of investment were created, aimed at promoting the activities of companies committed to looking for new solutions to sustainable development. Dignity, solidarity, equality, and

---

11 From *"Promoting a European Framework for Corporate Social Responsibility"*, a Green Paper by the European Commission, 18 July 2001.

defending those who are less respected, all become important parameters alongside environmental issues and safeguarding the planet's equilibrium. New behaviours are adopted where profit-making is placed alongside the safeguarding of human rights and an appreciation of operational methodologies, so that mankind and the market can develop in harmony. These new types of investment have rapidly gained ground in all countries with advanced economies.

Some of these new types of investment relate to the "theory of sustainable development". According to this theory, by extending their timescales, intermediaries and manufacturing companies are able to try to identify and/or assume some of the costs that are linked to so-called "market failures" – i.e., aspects which the market, over time, has been unable to automatically predict or manage – without betraying their support for the market's fundamental profit-making principles. The examples that belong to this category are not just those of environmental sustainability but, above all, respect for mankind's inalienable rights, including the right to health.

The general assumption of these new theories on the role of the company within the society where it operates is the recognition that its responsibilities include not only those towards its shareholders but also those towards many other individuals.[12] In fact, in addition to shareholders, stakeholders can also be identified as having specific interests in the company. These are private individuals or legal entities that, although they are not shareholders, have a legitimate interest

---

12   This is the Stakeholder Theory that was in total contrast with the Shareholder Theory, whereby the only obligation on the part of management is to increase company profits. The Stakeholder Theory was defined by R. Edward Freeman, Olsson Professor of Applied Ethics at the University of Virginia's Darden School.

in the conduct of the company. This is because its conduct, and any consequences thereof, can have an impact on them. A classic example of stakeholders are local communities which, although they do not have formal title to the company, are undoubtedly interested in its activities. One need only think about the potential repercussions of decisions made by a company in relation to local environment or local labour markets.

Even those who have a contractual relationship with the company can be considered stakeholders for anything that is not covered by applicable laws governing such contractual relationships. In this sense, employees, customers and suppliers are stakeholders too, because their interests extend beyond those safeguarded legally by their employment, purchasing and supply contracts respectively. Shareholders, too, can be considered stakeholders when they are at the receiving end of company conduct aimed at safeguarding their interests, unless this was contractually provided for. Consequently, complying with rules that define management and the control of a company, as well as transparency and accuracy of company information, becomes a duty for any ethical company. This, however, will be dealt with in later chapters.

Corporate social responsibility, in its various guises, has developed and become popular in the last few years and is currently widely recognised, accepted and applied. However, it is in total contrast with the neo-liberalist view of the economy, where, as maintained by Milton Friedman, the only responsibility of a company is towards its shareholders and of maximising profits.

In discussing social responsibility, it is worth stressing the risk that moral principles such as dignity, solidarity and equality are introduced into a company not so much according to any principle of ethics, but in line with the rules of marketing, which are based on the market welcoming and approving these ideas. Consequently, the company is rewarded with better economic and financial results. However, common sense leads us to believe that some of the initiatives that can be defined as "socially responsible" are merely motivated by increasing profit. In these cases they are a devious betrayal of ethical principles and cannot be considered "ethical" as defined in this guide.

② Ethics Applied to Economics

2.1 BEYOND ACCUMULATING WEALTH

As Adam Smith and other advocates of utilitarianism maintained, it is an unquestionable fact that self-interest is the fundamental motivation for man's willingness to work and do business. Nethertheless, the argument that self-interest can only be identified with accumulating wealth is excessively extremist and, therefore, unrealistic.

The groundlessness of this argument comes from various considerations that are briefly outlined in this section.

MAN EXPRESSES HIS OWN HUMANITY

In civil society, morals can be whittled down to their fundamental parts because everybody is free to decide not to comply with even basic moral principles as long as the law is not infringed. The same rationale does not apply to the business world because its essence includes some principles that can rightly be defined as ethical. Several international studies carried out by the Institute of Global Ethics, a non-profit association set up in the USA in the 1990s to educate and promote a debate on ethics, have shown that values such as trust, compassion, responsibility, freedom, respect for life and honesty are considered by the vast majority of people to be of fundamental importance in business and, consequently, they are recognised as such.[1] If it is taken into account that during the working day these values influence our moods and behaviour, it is easy to realise how they inevitably influence decisions that we make on a daily basis. Therefore, the rationale of the economic world is greatly influenced by the existence of these very values, and the belief that people can leave the business world completely exterior to feelings pertaining to their "humanity" is not credible.

A system centred around people, such as business, cannot realistically be analysed unless all the aspects pertaining to people themselves are taken into account: not just the strictly rational aspect at the base of a pursuance of self-interest, but also the non-rational aspect, where people find their motivation for business transactions in love, generosity, altruism, respect, trust, understanding, recognition, joy, and hope, as well as in greed, meanness, revenge, etc.

Consider the large dose of love and affection that goes into the economic choice of buying jewellery for a loved one. If, then, part of the decision comes from more rational grounds, such as the conviction that the piece of jewellery is an excellent investment and that, as such, it will acquire greater value in the future, this does not at all invalidate the argument that there are feelings involved which play a role even in the business world. Consider the measure of altruism

---

1 *Moral Courage*, Rushworth M. Kidder, William Morrow, 2005. Rushworth M. Kidder is the founder of the Institute of Global Ethics.

and generosity inherent in a donation to charity, or the amount of hope that is placed on a bet in the national lottery; or the measure of "infectious greed" (from the definition of Alan Greenspan, former Chairman of the US Federal Reserve) pervading the managers involved in the financial scandals at the beginning of the century. There are obviously countless examples. If it is accepted, therefore, that the irrational side of people plays an important role in the business world, it seems logical to assume that there is a moral and ethical aspect that needs to be considered, and that is not possible to turn a blind eye to it as has been done for long time.

ECONOMICS IS BORN WITH A SOCIAL FUNCTION

The fact that there are some ethical principles or values that characterise economics can be ascertained by analysing its origins. The development of modern economy originated from the desire to improve the living conditions of people and of society in general. In the past, all economic activities, including inventions, aimed to develop society, such that each of them actually led to an improvement in general living conditions. Economics brought with it general progress and wellbeing and, in this sense, it was ethical. Consider the discovery of penicillin by Sir Alexander Fleming, or the radio telegraph by Guglielmo Marconi. In those days, scientists and entrepreneurs were primarily motivated by the wish to find a cure for a disease or to solve a social problem, such as that of long-distance communication, and not so much by personal gain. The financial aspect was just one of the consequences of the success and fame they achieved. The impression is that nowadays this motivation keeps being the main drive only for some scientific researchers. Given the very low chances of success in research and the relatively modest salaries that researchers usually receive, it is in fact difficult to believe that financial considerations have great impact on their motivation. On the contrary, the drive for today's entrepreneurs and businessmen seems to be greatly shifted towards mere financial gain.

CIVIL SOCIETY CLAIMS THE ETHICAL FUNCTION OF ECONOMICS

The following are only some examples of the public's reaction to what it believed was the unethical conduct of some companies:

- At the end of the 1970s, Nestlé, the Swiss food multinational, was the subject of international criticism because it was using misleading marketing strategies to sell, particularly in developing countries, powdered milk as an alternative to breast milk. This milk was given away to hospitals for free and used to feed newborn babies to the detriment of breast feeding. When mothers left hospital, they found themselves in the situation of having to purchase artificial milk at a very high price which could even amount to half the family income. As they did not have any alternative, milk was often diluted with water causing newborn babies to be malnourished or poisoned if the water was not clean. In 1977, the criticism directed towards the company translated into an international boycott. In 2002, UNICEF claimed that Nestlé was violating the international code of the World Health Organisation, which prohibited the promotion of powdered milk to feed newborn babies.

- In the 1990s, there was outrage at the news that Nike, the US manufacturer of sports shoes and clothing, was using child labour for its manufacturing in developing countries, particularly Pakistan, and was paying salaries that were lower than the minimum wage allowed by law.

- Still in the 1990s, Dow Corning, a US group manufacturing breast implants among other products, faced multiple lawsuits because the implants were considered so harmful to women's health as to cause breast cancer.

- In 2007 Mattel Inc., the US company and one of the largest toy manufacturers in the world, had to recall more than twenty million toys manufactured in China because they were considered hazardous. The toys, in fact, contained lead-based paints which could release toxic substances if ingested.

In order to defend generally recognised moral values, civil society mobilises itself, even on an international scale. Compared to the past, investigative journalism and publishing of episodes considered unethical has increased and, as a consequence, violations of fundamental moral principles are today more likely to be brought to light. Moreover, a number of associations have been created with the mission to identify these types of violations and denounce them publicly.

There is no doubt that the aforementioned companies suffered from the consequences of their actions being brought to the knowledge of the general public.

- Nestlé has been the target of the longest boycott campaign ever towards a company. Obviously, it is impossible to ascertain the extent to which this campaign has affected and affects the reputation of the company and, ultimately, its sales. However, it would be logical to believe that the impact on sales has been significantly negative.

- In April 2005, Nike issued its first Corporate Responsibility Report disclosing its contract factory base manufacturing Nike-branded products in developing countries. This decision provided greater visibility into sub-contractors and more efficient monitoring by independent parties.[2]

- Dow Corning was forced to compensate an extremely high number of customers who had sued it. This virtually bankrupted the company in 1998. In the following years, a number of scientific studies showed the lack of connection between implants and any type of cancer or serious condition.[3]

- The way that the Mattel case ended and the recall of its toys has had an important symbolic consequence: an admission of guilt by the US company and a formal apology to the Chinese government and people. In September 2007, in fact, Mattel's top executives admitted that the mistake that had led to the recall of the toys was not attributable to Chinese production but to the design of the product by the American engineers of the group.[4]

Even though a number of socio-economic reasons, such as mass production, consumerism and globalisation, have weakened the link between the economy on the one hand and progress/ethicality on the other, civil society takes a position whenever the capitalist system does not apply recognised ethical principles. This supports the notion that ethics is an integral part of the economy.

---

2   See "Nike Inc. Issues 2004 Corporate Responsibility Report" on www. incr.com, April 13th, 2005.

3   See "Panel Confirms No Major Illness Tied to Implants", *The New York Times*, 21 June 1999.

4   See "Mattel Official Apologizes in China", *The New York Times*, 21 September 2007.

COMPANIES HAVE AN INSTITUTIONAL AND SOCIAL DIMENSION

In a free market, each company has an institutional and social dimension in addition to an economic dimension that pushes it to maximise shareholders' profits.

An institutional dimension means the fact that a business is the product, and subsequently the source, of a network of internal and external contracts (e.g., shareholders, employees, customers and suppliers), binding it to fulfil commitments that are hierarchically above the very quest for profit. These are, for instance, the tacit agreement with the State to pay taxes on time, or the commitment to staff and suppliers to pay salaries and purchase invoices respectively. Moreover, most companies providing basic services such as transport, logistics, electricity, water, civil engineering and public administration, play a role that is characterised by its objective value to the public with repercussions that are felt both inside and outside the companies themselves.

As well as the institutional dimension, a company also has a social dimension. A company is, in fact, a web of individuals, each with their own needs and aspirations, for whom the company is often the main tool for meeting those needs and achieving those aspirations. Should this not happen, the effects are felt at the level of people's satisfaction, which results in a deterioration of their quality of life. Furthermore, a company has a social function in that it is an integral part of the business world, which is basically a wide network of professional communities where the individual creates relationships with colleagues and third parties. In this sense, he builds a rich web of mutual expectations based typically on ethical trust, which would entail serious economic consequences if disregarded.

2.2 QUALIFYING THE CHARACTERISTICS OF ETHICS

As the concept of ethics is rather abstract and subjective, it can be defined in several ways. Therefore, it would be fruitless to attempt to find a definition of ethics that is more suited to the meaning used in this guide. Instead, identifying a series of characteristics within the notion of "ethics" would be of greater help.

SENSE OF RESPONSIBILITY

Being ethical, means, above all, being responsible, i.e., being aware of the fact that any decision, at any company level it is taken, has implications for one or few company stakeholders and that these implications could not be just economic in nature. The decisions to transfer manufacturing from one country to another, to close down a plant, to make an employee redundant can have strong ethical connotations because they have an impact on one or more individuals. Some decisions that have a direct impact on the environment, such as the construction of civil engineering works, the extraction of natural resources and deforestation activities, affect the health and quality of life of the communities in the area where these activities take place and, at times, have an impact even on the health and quality of life of society as a whole.

At times, the consequences of some decisions can be final in the sense that a return to the previous situation is difficult or unlikely. Still on the subject of the environment, pollution, activities generating or amplifying the greenhouse effect in the atmosphere with the ensuing overheating of the earth, and the deforestation of vast areas, as is the case in Amazonia, are examples of activities whose consequences are felt on the ecosystem of the world and whose damages are, in most cases, irreversible.

In relation to problems such as the mentioned ones, the need to be responsible is usually clear because the consequences would be particularly serious as an extraordinarily high number of people is affected. Although they are less visible to many people, even decisions made by companies on a daily basis can have serious consequences, and the financial and economic crisis of 2008 has very painfully shown this. In order to avoid taking on responsibility, the tendency within companies to adopt behaviour aimed at foregoing responsibility, such as delegating to others issues pertaining to one's own sphere of competence, prevaricating in situations that would need immediate action, taking wrong decisions motivated by a reluctance to disappoint interested parties, is very common.

To avoid situations in which responsibility for a company decision cannot be attributed to the individual who has taken it, a close relationship between the two components – the decision (or action) and its responsibility – needs to be established. Sometimes, this relationship is there but is not clear and therefore confusion ensues. Invariably, two issues arise in relation to this point:

1. Assigning responsibilities for the various types of decisions, that is, assigning specific organisational roles with adequate authority to the selected individuals, in a clear and agreed manner;

2. Selecting the people who, on the one hand, have the technical competencies and, on the other, have the personal maturity and ethical sense to take on their responsibilities.

To gain a better understanding of the importance of the notion of responsibility and how much this is ultimately connected with that of ethicality, let's consider a very realistic case that exemplifies similar situations which invariably presents themselves in any company.

A chief executive officer is a professional to whom shareholders delegate responsibility to manage the company in their own interests and in compliance with current laws and regulations. Let us now assume that he is asked to approve the acquisition of a company. From a technical point of view, this would be considered a correct move if the following two conditions are met:

1. The value and purchase price has been calculated with due diligence by a third party, i.e., someone who is independent both of the buyer and the seller; and

2. There is no conflict of interest involving the chief executive officer in that he has no interest in the operation that go beyond the interests related to his role as an administrator. He could find himself in this situation if, for instance, he were a partner of the company being acquired. If this were the case, he would do his utmost to get the buying company to pay a price that was higher than the appropriate one because, in so doing, his personal gains as shareholder of the acquired company would increase.

However, let us assume that these, normally legal, requirements are met. Does the chief executive officer act with propriety when he approves an acquisition without evaluating all the circumstances and adequately consulting the company assurance function so that the decision turns out to be not in line with company strategy? Clearly, the answer is no.

However, the conduct of the chief executive officer is unlikely to be punished because this moral duty – being responsibly informed – is not often reflected expressly in law, and his guilt is difficult to prove. As with countless situations in life, the dilemma transforms itself from a legal problem (adherence to express formal laws) to a moral issue. Therefore, the chief executive officer in this example is definitely guilty from an ethical standpoint because his role is to safeguard the interests of the shareholders who, in this instance, would end up losing out to an investment that is not strategically justified.

In the business world, the duty of those who hold positions rightly defined "of responsibility" is always to take on this responsibility. Since it is impossible to regulate in detail every situation that could arise in real life, the law is, by definition, limited because there are and there will always be situations that are not regulated, situations for which there is a legislative "hole" or for which the relevant laws can be construed in different ways. However, if *a priori* it has been rationally agreed that the chief executive officer is responsible for always managing the company in the shareholders' interests, then he will have to shoulder the same responsibility even when this aspect is not captured by the law, the only difference being that a legal obligation is replaced by a moral one. A wise and intellectually honest person will continue to consider a moral obligation as if it had the same coercive force as a legal obligation because the background has not changed.

How many times, following a financial scandal, do journalists and magistrates ask CEOs and managers the typical question "Why was this situation, with a high risk of fraud, not previously brought to light?" and the answer they invariably receive is "we did not know about it" or "we were not told about it"? Every time the chief executive officer has to make a decision that is binding on the company, he cannot get away from finding out sensibly about circumstances that required that decision to be made, the factors that somehow influence it and the implications it could have both within and outside the company. He has to be able to express an opinion on the legality and ethicality of all critical company decisions and cannot hide behind the argument that he was not informed of this or that situation. Obviously, this is not an easy task, but this is the reason why those who shoulder this level of responsibility are remunerated with generous packages, significantly higher than those who do not bear similar responsibilities.

HONOUR THE TRUST

The business world has always been based, in particular, on trust in others. In the past, loans were granted merely on the strength of one's word since legal guarantees were not in use. Bartering too was based on mutual trust because the exchange could not always take place at the same time. Nowadays, the mechanisms and techniques for carrying out economic transactions are very different. Nonetheless, the notion of trust continues to be a necessary requirement for these transactions to come to fruition. If trust towards an individual were not there, no-one would dare make any transaction, or work on a project or carry out any other work-related activity with another individual. Even if at the root of these transactions there were a contract signed by the parties involved, the situation would not change substantially because the existence of a contract, or at any rate a legal document, is not in itself sufficient to guarantee that the other party is going to fulfil its obligations. Ultimately, only the level of trust that we feel towards the other party will convince us to take on the related risks.

In business, therefore, individuals continuously place their trust in other individuals. Consequently the latter are selected not only on their skills but also on their ability to honour the trust that has been placed in them by their counterparts. This aspect is commonly considered an essential requirement inherent in the notion of professionalism. For some professions, this is expressly decreed by their association's code of ethics. Consider, for instance, the principle of client confidentiality as recognised by various professional bodies in, for example, medicine and law, and as laid down in their respective professional codes.

The importance of honouring this relationship of trust can also be perceived in the dramatic consequences to the economy when this trust is betrayed. In 2001, the Houston office of the international auditing company Arthur Andersen was involved in the bankruptcy of the US multinational Enron. Arthur Andersen was found guilty of having certified for years the group's financial statements even though they did not truthfully represent the business and financial position of their client. Moreover, once the enquiry started, the auditors physically got rid of the documents that evidenced their awareness of the disastrous situation of their client. Over a period of just a few months, the national subsidiaries of this international auditing network lost most of their clients. In a dramatic domino effect, the entire international network of Arthur Andersen went bankrupt and its brand that for a century was synonymous with recognised professionalism, vanished from the global scene.

DEMONSTRATION OF MORAL COURAGE

The ability to take on responsibility for ethics is closely linked to the amount of courage that is available and that develops over time. Normally, people with no morals or scruples thrive because they are not thwarted by people who are ethical but lack the courage to show it. As in real life, superstar culture leads people to be judged more by success, power and money than on the basis of their principles, lifestyle and life choices from which they draw inspiration. In some cases there is a tendency to sympathise with immorality rather than oppose it. Individuals are ethical particularly when they have the courage to take a stance against those who do not behave ethically by condemning them openly too. In this regard, Rushworth M. Kidder, who in 1990 founded the Institute for Global Ethics in the USA, wrote:

> *Moral courage is not about facing physical challenges that could harm the body. It's about facing mental challenges that could harm one's reputation, emotional well-being, self-esteem, or other characteristics.*

Kidder points out that people often identify moral courage as one of the main virtues alongside honesty, respect, responsibility, fairness and compassion. However, he adds something to its definition that sets it apart from other virtues:

> *Rather than being the next pearl on a string... moral courage is something that enables the others to be effective. Maybe it's the string itself. Maybe it's the catalyst that speeds up the reaction times of the*

*others... it is the greatest of all virtues; because, unless
a man has that virtue, he has no security for preserving
any other.* [5]

Every organisation and association involved in the fight
against company fraud agrees in stating that most crimes
would have been avoided or, at least, discovered before
they were committed, if someone within the company
had asked the right questions at the right time. As in life, a
critical attitude must be adopted in companies vis-à-vis what
happens around us. One must always have the courage to ask
questions whenever something is not clear or convincing.
Investigative literature clearly defines this attitude as "healthy
scepticism".

TOOL TO ACHIEVE COMPANY OBJECTIVES

Ethicality is not a luxury that can be afforded during those
periods when the economic climate is positive and financial
results are satisfactory and then, during lean periods, is put
aside and far less orthodox business choices are not sniffed
at. Apart from characterising the individuals belonging to a
company, ethicality must be a deeply rooted characteristic
of a company; it must characterise each behaviour of
the organisation so as to be consistent over time and not
influenced by external factors like the economic trends of the
market in which it operates. In this sense, one-off initiatives
with a humanitarian and anthropological slant, increasingly
undertaken by businesses in the wake of society's increased
awareness towards social responsibility, do not fulfil the
responsibility that companies have. These initiatives are often
undertaken because they are considered a rather efficient low-

---

5   *Moral Courage*, an essay by Rushworth M. Kidder published by the
Institute for Global Ethics in 2005.

cost advertising tool since they play on people's consciences and induce lofty feelings, such as generosity and altruism. Less frequently, these initiatives are sincerely prompted by altruistic intentions and, as such, they represent decidedly positive and desirable behaviour. Even when prompted by genuine intentions, these initiatives have little to do with the company ethics, i.e., what an organisation expresses in its conduct and in decisions taken by its members whilst carrying out their daily tasks, those which are instrumental to achieving the goals formally set out in the company's mission and strategy. Therefore, an organisation's ethicality is not the one expressed in undertaking initiatives independent from the company's normal activity but the one systematically and continuously reflected in all the daily activities the organisation carries out and to accomplish which it was originally created.

In 1991, Gianni Agnelli, deceased grandson of the founder of the Italian automotive group FIAT, and then chairman of FIAT, group that in 2009 merged with Chrysler, the US car manufacturer, to create the second largest automotive group, stated on ethics that:[6]

> *In the specific case of managing a company, we are continuously making choices involving our relationships with employees, shareholders, competition and the State. These choices cannot be limited only to considerations of an economic nature, but they inevitably lead us towards ethics. And we know that complying with laws is not enough to fully define the social usefulness of the goals that we set and the moral lawfulness of the means that we use:*

---

6   *"Valori e sviluppo"* (Values and Development) in *"L'etica da applicare"* (The Ethics to Apply) by Armando Massarenti and Antonio Da Re, Il Sole 24 Ore Libri 1991.

it is an ongoing audit that we must carry out within ourselves, a permanent comparison between the principles we make reference to and the reality that shows itself to be different according to the case.[7]

Therefore, it is an ongoing effort that the company must make to ensure that ethically proper decisions are constantly made from within. It is not an easy task because in ethics there are few certainties. One must question oneself continuously to identify the most acceptable solution. This commitment must involve the whole company because, irrespective of our positions, we all make company-related choices that invariably have an ethical implication, though final responsibility lies with the board of directors.

---

7   "*Valori e sviluppo*" (Values and Development) in *L'etica da applicare* (The Ethics to Apply) by Armando Massarenti and Antonio Da Re, Il Sole 24 Ore Libri 1991.

"The chief value of money lies in the fact that one lives in a world in which it is overestimated."

> Henry Louis Mencken 1880–1956,
> US journalist and critic

"Where there is no vision, the people perish."

> Ancient proverb

"To see what is right and not to do it is want of courage."

> Confucius 551 B.C. – 479 B.C.,
> (Dialogues, Book II, Chapter XXIV)

"The Earth has enough for everyone's need, but not enough for everyone's greed."

> Mahatma Gandhi 1869–1948

"The superior man understands what is right; the inferior man understands what will sell."

> Confucius 551 B.C. – 479 B.C.,
> (Dialogues, Book IV, Chapter XVI)

3 The Roots of Ethical Uncertainty: A Change in Values

3.1 THE SUPERSTAR CULTURE

There are various reasons for which the business world has started to think in distinctly individualistic terms and to give less importance to its social context which, undoubtedly, was the inspiration for the birth of economics. Today, commitment to work and, therefore, business management, is only thought of as a function of the gain that can be derived. This belief, however, causes a real loss of the meaning of work. Albert Einstein suggested that:

> *One should guard against preaching success to young people in the customary form of it being the main aim in life. The most important motive for work in school and in life is the pleasure in work, pleasure in*

its result, and the knowledge of the value of the result
to the community.

In March 2005, Richard Layard, distinguished economist at
the London Business School, stated:

We live in an age of unprecedented individualism.
The highest obligation many people feel is to make
the most of themselves, to realise their potential... Of
course they feel obligations to other people too, but
these are not based on any clear set of ideas. The old
religious worldview is gone; so, too, is the post-war
religion of social and national solidarity. We are left
with no concept of the common good or of collective
meaning... and every successful society has always
concerned itself with the tastes of its members. It has
encouraged community feelings and offered a concept
of the common good.[1]

Identifying what has caused this change over the years is
rather difficult as there are a number of factors which, over
time, have affected it. Nevertheless, the main reasons are
related to the notion of culture and, in particular, its various
components: moral values; lifestyles; habits; customs; and
laws, just to mention a few. Each one of them has changed
over time and has led to their harmonisation across different
countries, peoples, races and religions. This harmonisation
has been facilitated, especially in the economic sector, by
globalisation. The mass media has played a crucial role in the
process of "universalising" culture and the change in values
and moral references, effected through the uniformity of their

---

1   From Richard Layard's articles published in the magazine *Prospect* in
March 2005.

messages and through the exaltation of consumerism by the repeated use of advertising.

Over the last few years, the mass media has become very efficient in addressing the public's thinking and lifestyle. Television, in particular, has turned out to be the most suitable medium to disseminate values, ideas and fads that are assimilated and made their own by modern society, and new generations in particular, at an unthinkable speed. Moreover, the use of the "small screen" has now reached astonishing levels: according to the most recent studies in the UK the television consumption has reached 3.8 hours a day; while in the US it has peaked 5 hours a day.[2] The wide use of television has added to its effectiveness as a means of communication, amplifying its effects on the behaviour and mentality of the general public. Nowadays it would be unthinkable to sell a product without a high budget to advertise it through the media, and particularly through television. Over time there has been a change in the values the media portrays and those that are being shown today seem to match those of the "superstar theory" developed by Kirk O. Hanson, director of the Markkula Center for Applied Ethics based in California. This theory is based on the glorification of the winner to the denigration and humiliation of others.[3] At the 1996 Atlanta Olympics, one of Nike's adverts trumpeted: "You do not win silver, you lose gold". This message was in sharp contrast with that of Pierre de Coubertin, founder of the modern Olympic Games, who in 1896 stated: "The most important thing is not to win but to take part".

---

2   For the UK see 2008 Ofcom report, for US. see Nielsen 4th Quarter 2008 "Three Screen Report".

3   The superstar culture was defined by Kirk O. Hanson, professor of Applied Ethics at Santa Clara University in the USA.

There are many examples of celebrities in any sector of social life, from art to music, from sport to business, who are created and kept alive by the media so that they always have material to fill their TV and radio programmes, newspapers and magazine columns. A direct consequence of this is the growing popularity of tabloids, whose content is almost exclusively that of photographic images of superstars, and articles analysing totally insignificant details of their public and private lives, often with no respect for their privacy. Sportsmen like Tiger Woods, Michael Schumacher, Andre Agassi and David Beckham are so acclaimed and celebrated by the media that they have become real celebrities, recognised by everyone anywhere in the world, and loved by everybody. To prove this, the vast majority of the very high fees that these people earn comes from lavish sponsorship deals and their work giving testimonials in advertising campaigns for all sorts of products. The same holds true for actors, singers and models: only a handful of the "chosen few" have international coverage and they are the only ones entitled to success, recognition, attention, esteem, envy and, obviously, wealth.

Over the last few years, this superstar culture has characterised the business world too. The top managers of large multinationals are now considered fully-fledged celebrities. Very rarely are the financial statements of a group with an internationally recognised brand presented without a picture of its Chief Executive Officer on the front cover smoking a cigar or shaking hands with someone. It is no longer clear if this way of releasing financial statements aims at publicising the companies' activities and results, or whether it is a way of increasing their CEOs' popularity. In 2005, Peter Bakker, the Dutch CEO of TNT, at the time one of the largest players in the sector of mail, logistics and transport, invited Bono, the famous lead singer of the band U2, to the annual meeting of its general directors. The previous year, he had been interviewed by Larry King, the very well-known CNN journalist.

3.2 CONSEQUENCES OF THE SUPERSTAR CULTURE

The popularity of superstar culture is a worrying feature of modern society. Since it is founded on a short-term vision, it leads people to think in purely selfish and individualistic terms. Its application to the business world, and in particular the lack of long-term vision that characterises it, means that the economic system is facing the risk of declining, if not collapsing. The financial crisis of 2008 is, to a certain extent, a consequence of the popularity of this culture based on consumerism and materialism pushed to the extreme. In order to feed itself, the system has, on the one hand, pushed individuals and families to contract a high level of debt, and on the other, led financial institutions to deal with these ever increasing levels of indebtedness by taking on greater risks, totally without thought in some cases.

The increased popularity of this culture is also the origin and consequence of the adoption of remuneration systems and incentives which generate unthinkable levels of wealth. This means that an increasing number of individuals are enormously wealthy. The consequence is that these people, whose lives are based on luxury and appearances, become negative role models for civil society, which often takes them – more or less unconsciously – as examples to follow because it does not have adequate discerning skills.

The type of culture to promote should not therefore be one that is founded on levels of wealth and success achieved but one that encourages those who do their best and strive to use their skills and talents in an intelligent and constructive fashion. It should be a culture that appreciates those who, with a less individualistic approach, try to contribute to the development of society and to defend its long-term sustainability.

George Soros is considered to be the guru of world finance and the greatest speculator of all time. On his own, he can bring the economy of an entire nation, or its currency at least, to its knees. He became particularly famous when in 1992 he earned $1 billion by speculating on the devaluation of the Italian lira, thus becoming one of the richest men on earth.

The following observation he made in a 1997 interview describes the consequences of the superstar culture quite well:

> *In Adam Smith's days, capitalist economic theories combined with moral philosophy. Market values were used to push away other traditional values. However, as the market mechanism was growing, these values have been abandoned. Increasingly, people consider money a value. Anything that costs more is considered to be better. People only respect you because you are rich. The cult of success has replaced faith in principles. Laissez faire has banned the redistribution of wealth.*[4]

Society frequently runs after the most celebrated superstar of the moment and, because one of the things they unfailingly share is the fact that they have lots of money, this becomes the means to gain others' respect, the objective to pursue in life.

---

4   George Soros in *Avvenimenti*, 5 February 1997.

The popularity of this superstar culture has some significant and, at the times, dangerous consequences on society, which are described in the following pages.

CONCENTRATION OF WEALTH AND POWER

In 2007, before the financial crisis which hit the assets of the super rich too, according to the yearly list drawn up by the American economic magazine *Forbes*, there were 1,125 dollar billionaires. Considering that in 2003, the same list had 587 of them, this means that in only 5 years this number has almost doubled this corresponding to a 19 per cent average increase each year. Their combined net worth in 2007 amounted to $4.4 trillion, a 132 per cent increase compared to 2003 and a 26 per cent increase compared to 2006. According to the same source, in 2007 the CEOs of the major 500 US companies received a total combined remuneration of $6.4 billion, an individual average of $12.8 million and a 48 per cent increase on 2003.[5]

Obviously, these are astronomical figures that have little or nothing to do with most people's average salary. According to the same US statistics, in 1980, CEOs of US multinationals on average earned about 40 times the average salary of their employees whereas in 1990, they earned 100 times as much, and in 2006 about 400 times as much. These statistics highlight the worrying tendency of global wealth to be concentrated in the hands of a few individuals.

---

5   Data from the 2007 lists of "The World's Billionaires" and "Top Paid CEOs", *Forbes Magazine*.

Speaking about the financial crisis which hit the global economy in 2008, A. C. Grayling, writer and professor of philosophy at the Birkbeck College in London, stated that:

> *The gap between the rich and the rest is very large and, in the credit-fuelled economies of the last 15 years, has grown hugely. Recognising that the wealth of the mega-rich too often comes at the expense of others, and that great wealth can be more productive of problems than happiness – a familiar point, but it takes a longish recession to help people understand with their intestines as well as their heads that money and happiness are not automatic partners – will assuredly refocus attention on the things whose value and price are not only not the same thing, but very different things.*[6]

There is a close correlation between wealth and power. Wealth entails, at the very least, easy access to power, whatever type of power that may be. Thirst for power inevitably goes through thirst for wealth and this dangerously increases psychological pressure to increase personal wealth without too many scruples. All means become legitimate when trying to reach the goal of becoming wealthier, and to such an extent that any sense of proportion can be lost, as people no longer realise the illegitimacy of their behaviour.

The combination of wealth and power also entails other risks for the economic system. A classic example is monopolies. At the end of the 1990s, the American software giant, Microsoft, founded and led by Bill Gates, currently one of the richest people in the world, was accused by the federal government

---

6   From "Greed Is No Longer Good", A. C. Grayling, *The Sunday Telegraph*, 4 January 2009.

and many US states of using anti-competitive methods to keep its monopoly on computer operating systems, and of trying to monopolise the market for browsers (the software which enables navigation through the Internet).

These monopolies cause serious harm to the economy and, ultimately, to consumers who are forced to pay artificially high prices. Companies with a monopoly in fact exploit the limited risk of losing their own clients, who would have to forego the acquisition of a good or service, to impose prices that are higher than those that would otherwise be economically justifiable. Sometimes, the Anti-Trust Authorities, which are responsible for overseeing the business world in order to prevent monopolies or, at any rate, anti-competitive practices, fail and so allow this type of fraud to take place. Monopolistic business models are, perhaps, a more devious type of fraud because they are particularly difficult to identify and they are at the detriment of the general public as a whole. Clearly, their existence makes the entire economic system less transparent and efficient.

DISPARITY BETWEEN SALARIES AND INEQUALITY

Another consequence of the superficial and materialistic culture portrayed by the image of the superstar is the unjustified disparity between salaries that it has created. Consider the salary of a schoolteacher, which is a fraction of the salary of a TV presenter or a football player. At best a presenter, when he is good, cheers us up for a few hours but does not have a long-lasting impact on our quality of life. Equally, society neither improves nor worsens as a result of the competitive level reached by the national football league. On the other hand, society's development is strongly influenced by the quality of its teachers and educators.

The objective should be that of stressing the correlation between salary levels and the contribution that remunerated human activities or professions make to society's progress and welfare. In so doing, we would make the most of the existing inventory of skills and talents in a given society in any given period of time, maximising the level of progress and ensuring the best possible quality of life for each member of society. If remuneration does not reflect the added value given to the good of society, not only is society's progress hindered but it paves the way for conflicting situations which can be more or less latent in the short term but, in the long term, could well degenerate. History, even recent history, is full of examples of this type.

SENSE OF IMPUNITY

Following the discovery of fraud perpetrated by Giampiero Fiorani, the chief executive of Banca Popolare Italiana, the Italian journalist Michele Serra described the position of absolute power and feeling of impunity in which the accused had found himself when handling the bank accounts of his clients with total discretion:

> *Impunity: in my opinion this is the real added value of power, and what makes it irresistible and, at the same time, ruinous. From a certain point it feels as if you have become a member of an elite which no longer abides by common rules, and which can create its own rules. You either have the moral strength to withstand the climate of inebriating conceit in which you find yourself beyond that point, or you are not even aware that what you are doing is illegal and that you are riding roughshod over other people's rights. I imagine that moral qualms among those with power*

(especially those with financial power) are almost unutterable, as if such qualms were from a world far away. The loss of any sense of limit goes hand in hand with the geometric progression of success and wealth: if I have come this far, it means that I could make it, and that I was right. Giampiero Fiorani is said to be lost in jail, that he is trying to put his thoughts in order. It must be a terrible struggle: believing for years that he was almighty and above common judgement, and then suddenly finding himself in a position where he has to comply with rules that he has completely forgotten. Perhaps they were learnt in childhood but swallowed subsequently by life.[7]

Bernard Lawrence Madoff, US entrepreneur and former head of the NASDAQ stock market, must have found himself in a similar situation to the one just described when, on 12 March 2009, he was found guilty of financial fraud. In 1960 Madoff founded Bernard L. Madoff Investment Securities LLC, a financial company which carried out through a Ponzi scheme (in which no return on the investments of its customers was actually made but was paid by newly acquired customers), the largest fraud in history by a single individual. Investigators have in fact calculated that Madoff's clients lost a total of about $65 billion. During the years when Madoff was committing this fraud, he was able to escape every check by creating the necessary collusion with individuals working for the financial watchdogs. At the same time, he was leading a very peaceful life in luxury and comfort. In this case too, the power that money gave this individual meant that he developed a sense of impunity which made the situation even worse, so much

---

7   From "L'Amaca" di Michele Serra, *La Repubblica*, 22 December 2005.

so that this fraud continued for a number of years reaching unimaginable proportions.

By embodying success, power and money to the nth degree, these personalities are easily turned into legends by the public. This means a more or less conscious loss of objectivity in evaluating their work and morality. Surprisingly, there are some CEOs who carry on being stars and hold their positions at the top of their companies, still respected and venerated by everyone, despite having not achieved expected business results, or having implemented strategies that turned out to be disastrous for their companies.

Sir Fred Goodwin, former CEO of Royal Bank of Scotland, had to retire in 2008 when the bank's losses were such that the UK government had to nationalise it. When he left, he obtained a £16 million pension pot and a yearly pension of £650,000. Similarly, the top management of AIG, the American insurance giant, received several tens of millions of dollars as bonuses even though in autumn 2008 the US Administration had nationalised the company following its huge losses. Given the dramatic nature of the financial crisis at the time, in both cases the public asked their respective governments to provide official explanations. However, in a more favourable economic climate, similar events are likely to go unnoticed.

A CONTRASTING SOCIETY

A society in which, if you are not first you are considered a loser, ultimately leads its members to interact not on the basis of skills but of techniques that typify the practice of social climbing and the abuse of power. This mentality would generate a society where people are constantly clashing among themselves and, therefore, a type of society which is not sustainable and is morally disgraceful. Competition, as a formidable motivational lever in creating progress, is a constituent element of capitalism. However, when it only draws inspiration from the Machiavellian principle of the end justifying the means, it leads to immoral practices aimed at abusing others in a shortsighted attempt to be "first" at any cost. Hence, from a constructive element it becomes a destructive element in business and society. The very value of belonging to social or economic groups, where organised work carried out by more people gives better results than the sum of the activities of each individual, would be lost because no-one would be prepared to play secondary roles any longer. People who are inclined to play these roles would soon feel frustrated and dissatisfied because they would quickly realise that society sees them as losers and, as such, not worthy of respect and consideration.

(4) Ethical Risk and How to Manage It

4.1 THE FRAUD TRIANGLE THEORY

In order to gain a perception of ethical risk in relation to a specific organisation, it is useful to understand the psychological mechanisms that drive men, by nature selfish and greedy, to adopt unethical conduct.

We can be assisted to this end by the "fraud triangle" theory[1] which, even though it was developed in the field of criminology, is still equally valid when applied to the more general field of ethics. Before describing this theory, it is necessary to point out that fraud is just one aspect of a lack of ethics. A fraudster, in fact, is a person who is unethical in the sense that he has not adhered to the relevant legal framework, while people can be unethical while observing laws and rules. Nonetheless, in the remainder of this chapter, most references and discussions

---

1   The theory on the causes of fraud was developed by Donald R. Cressey (1919–1987). It is known as the "fraud triangle" where each element (psychological pressure, opportunity and rationalisation) constitutes a side of the triangle. This theory is described in *Other People's Money: A Study in the Social Psychology of Embezzlement* (1953).

will refer to fraud and, more precisely, to occupational fraud. Occupational fraud consists in the use of one's occupation for personal enrichment through the deliberate misuse or misapplication of the employing organization's resources or assets. The reference to occupational fraud is explained by the fact that fraud is more easily identifiable than unethical behaviour because it is a type of conduct that falls within a precise category as it is lack of compliance with laws and rules. As a consequence, its developments and trends are more easily monitored and measured over time thus offering a foundation on which to base the discussions that will be developed.

According to the fraud triangle theory, the risk of consciously adopting unethical behaviour is significantly high when the following three elements co-exist:

1. Psychological pressure;

2. Opportunity;

3. Rationalisation.

PSYCHOLOGICAL PRESSURE

Psychological pressure, or incentive, means all the factors which cause stress. An excessive amount of work, very heavy responsibilities, lack of support and guidance, a difficult working environment, and lack of professional fulfilment are just some of the possible motivations. Psychological pressure can also come from situations that have nothing to do with one's working environment: particularly expensive hobbies or habits, such as collecting vintage cars, or gambling, can become a source of tension unless the need for money that they entail is met.

OPPORTUNITY

Opportunity is the ease with which an individual can elude his company's internal controls. An internal control is a process that the management and control bodies of a company introduce because it supports the attainment of company objectives in terms of efficiency and effectiveness of operations, reliability of financial communication and compliance with laws and regulations.

RATIONALISATION

Rationalisation is the third element of the fraud triangle theory and is the ability to justify to oneself a behaviour that the individual knows is not morally correct. The ability to rationalise depends on the individual's personality and character which, in turn, are heavily influenced by the individual's own ethics. Since the individual is aware of the negative nature of his actions, he comes up with justifications for his behaviour in the hope that such an attempt will render it more acceptable to his own eyes. This is the mental process that the individual follows to feel less guilty and find the courage to take a morally questionable action.

The co-existence of psychological pressure, opportunity and rationalisation is a necessary condition for unethical conduct. On careful reflection, one cannot deny that these three components are also "sufficient" conditions in the sense that, if psychological pressure and opportunity co-exist in a given moment, only a balance between them and our ethical sense will prevent an unethical action. Our ethical principles, in fact, exercise an opposing force towards the other two components. However, this force has a limit beyond which the balance is lost and the individual's moral barriers come down. Hence, it is safe to assume that for any individual, however ethical he might be, there will always be a situation where he will start to rationalise and engage in deplorable behaviour. This is the kind of circumstance that is described by the peremptory and cynical yet very realistic saying "every man has his price". Furthermore, experience tells us that, if the limit beyond which people start to rationalise is exceeded, over time people will tend to move the goal post forward and commit increasingly unethical actions and even real crimes.

In the rest of this chapter, each of the three components of the criminal theory outlined above will be reviewed with a two-fold objective:

1. To analyse what is happening in companies today; and

2. To identify the most sensitive aspects requiring attention in an attempt to contain the problem of ethical uncertainty in business.

4.2 PSYCHOLOGICAL PRESSURE TO ACHIEVE

Psychological pressure is usually due to the appeal that money exerts on the modern man. Given the social pressure brought to bear by superstar culture, making money has become one's main preoccupation and activity on which to concentrate one's energy. Our lifestyle and quality of life are heavily influenced by this. Achievement and social respect have now become two variables directly proportional to our bank accounts.

In the era of the global economy, great wealth is created in the financial markets and in those sectors taking part in the "feasts" of large financial transactions. Consequently, the main objective of many young people is to find a job in one of these profitable sectors. However, a business degree is not enough, to the extent that a Masters in Business Administration (MBA) obtained from a handful of internationally renowned business schools is now an indispensable requirement to enter a career that can provide financial satisfaction. However, pocketing the right MBA is not exactly financially or psychologically cheap. In 2008 Harvard Business School, perhaps the most prestigious American University, received 8,661 applications and accepted only 12 per cent[2] of applicants. Similar acceptance levels can be found in the top 20 US and European business schools. Applicants who are accepted can expect 12 to 23 months of intense studying and fierce competition to achieve the best marks that will guarantee job offers from the best banks, consultancy firms, law firms or international industrial groups, all employers who guarantee fast and brilliant careers linked to generous salaries. However, there is a consequence for those who embark on this path of definite success and wealth which does not always receive due attention: the continuous and extraordinary pressure to perform.

Starting from the 1990s, in order to avoid risks linked to the previously discussed agency theory formulated by Adam Smith, an attempt was made to align top management's interests with those of major shareholders by linking their earnings to the performance of the company.[3] The solution that was found consisted of using the following tools as incentives and remuneration for executives:

---

2   From http://www.hbs.edu/about/statistics/.
3   *Ethics and Finance*, Avinash D. Persaud and John Plender, Longtail 2007, p. 9.

1. The bonus, whose value depends on some contractually agreed factors but is primarily linked to the financial results of the company; and

2. Stock options, a financial product enabling executives to buy company shares at a pre-determined price and to sell them on the market making a profit if the selling price exceeds the purchase price.

Therefore, the higher the company's profits (or rather "accounting" profits, that is those shown by its financial statements), the better its valuation in the financial markets and the more its executives earn both as a bonus and from stock options. Due to the different risk profile of the investments made by financial institutions compared to those made by manufacturing or service companies, the bonus, as a fair system to compensate company executives, loses its rationale.

In fact, in the financial sector and particularly in investment banking, executives can select investments with a higher than average risk profile so to generate higher profits. Investments that generate profits in the short term, may disclose themselves as being unprofitable when their consolidated results are considered on their lifetime. As a result of this, banks can suffer significant losses caused by investments that have generated previously "temporary" profits and on the basis of which generous bonuses were calculated and distributed to the bankers. The risk, as shown by the 2008 financial crisis, is that such a compensation system becomes a lethal incentive to do business at any cost, regardless of the risks involved. In autumn 2008, the US investment bank Lehman Brothers went bankrupt under management of its CEO, Richard Fuld. Even though the bank generated significant losses linked to the company exposure to the sub-prime mortgage market, Richard Fuld received total remuneration of $466 million in the years immediately before the bank's collapse.[4]

Anchoring bonuses to short-term profits means that this type of remuneration is often particularly significant and can exceed the fixed salary by 5, 10 or even 20 times. The result is that there are bankers who receive extraordinary remuneration. Between 2003 and 2006, Henry Paulson, who served as the 74th US Treasury Secretary and former C.E.O. of the investment bank Goldman Sachs, received a total amount of incentives in excess of $111 million.[5] In 2007, the five most important investment banks in Wall Street paid about $66 billion in salaries and remuneration, $39 billion of which was in bonuses. This meant average remuneration per employee of $353,000 including a $211,000 bonus.[6] At the time this book is being published, the large banks which survived the financial crisis, some of them bailed-out by governments, such as Royal Bank of Scotland in the UK owned by 84 per cent by the State, are announcing record-bonuses to be distributed to the bank employees.

Unlike company executives and bankers, the earnings of professionals who operate in international legal and strategic consultancy networks are closely linked to the number of hours they work for and devote to clients. Hence, to ensure high salaries, they need to sacrifice as much time as possible for their professions. Consequently, this type of company operates 24/7 to ensure that, for instance, there is always suitable

---

4   Reuters, 12 September 2008. The compensation of 466 million dollars refers to the period from 1993 to 2007, of the overall compensation stock options accounted for 363 million.
5   Bloomberg, 26 September 2008.
6   Bloomberg, 26 September 2008.

staff in Europe to answer a phone call from a client who is calling in the middle of the night from Japan. For consultants, therefore, working 15 hours a day and, periodically, entire nights in the office is the norm. This working pace, however, pushes psychological pressure to extraordinarily high levels and the limit beyond which rationsalisation takes place gets worryingly close.

Within the service and manufacturing industries, psychological pressure on the company managers comes from the assessment of results they have achieved on the basis of previously defined targets. At the beginning of the year, managers agree with their line managers a number of targets and commit themselves to reaching them during the year. The increase in the managers' salaries will, therefore, be closely related to the attainment of the targets. Usually, because career advancement is based on the same assessment method, tension to reach previously defined and agreed targets is particularly strong.

In short, to arrive at the top of the business pyramid, people have to be prepared to make huge sacrifices and withstand continuous and increasing psychological pressure. But what and who is at the top of the pyramid today? Over the last few years, the popularity of hedge funds has enjoyed a very fast increase. These are relatively unregulated investment funds whose philosophy is to achieve positive results irrespective of how the financial markets in which they operate are doing. Usually, this is achieved by short selling to reduce the price of securities. These funds need an enormous amount of capital which is usually borrowed. In some cases, they manage to invest up to $50 that they have borrowed for each dollar that is actually invested. Each year, this type of fund handles approximately $1,800 billion. There is no need to be an expert, therefore, to understand the huge risks involved in their use and popularity. Nonetheless, given the staggering rewards, managers of these funds easily forget the risks involved. For most of them, $100 million is the salary not for a year's work but that of a month. In 2007, $3 billion was the amount earned by John Paulson, the manager who tied in first place on the annual list of the 100 most successful speculators on Wall Street Stock Exchange, published by *Trader Monthly*, the American specialist magazine.[7] Phil Falcone, second on the list, earned between $1.5 billion and $2 billion. To be part of the group, you had to earn at least $75 million and six traders recorded earnings in excess of a billion of dollars. However, this is a profitable sector not only for the best but also for anyone who is fortunate enough to join this financial élite. In fact, even the salary of a graduate who has just started out in this sector exceeds $100,000. From there on, the sky is the limit.[8]

The sums at stake, therefore, create unprecedented psychological pressure to do business without considering whether it was good, and this situation, as history has shown us, leads to high risk situations. If an individual's ethics are not sufficiently strong to counteract the increased psychological pressure, the individual will rationalise the situation and will be driven to behave unethically. Since the 1990s, incentives such as bonuses and stock options have led various managers to falsify their company's financial statements or to carry out extraordinary financial operations that were not dictated by business motivation but to influence an increase in their own remuneration. This system was also one of the main reasons

---

7   "The Trader Monthly 100" published by the US magazine *Trader*, hedge funding section, April 2007 (the top 100 trader list is not available for 2008: on February 3, 2009, the magazine's publisher ended the *Trader Monthly's* operations).
8   See *Institutional Investor's Alpha*, the magazine specialised in hedge funding.

for some of the financial scandals that were unearthed at the beginning of the millennium, while the abused system of bonuses in the banking sector was one of the main factors that unleashed the financial crisis of 2008.

Therefore, it is worth pointing out that, on the one hand, incentives are necessary to motivate people and to reward their work according to meritocratic criteria.

On the other hand, they create unprecedented psychological pressure and expose the entire economic and financial system to enormous previously unknown risks. The financial crisis of 2008, ongoing at the time of writing, will stress this tendency and contribute to the further increasing psychological pressure felt, for instance, by those who are losing their jobs or those who, because they are insolvent, have to turn their homes over to the banks. The Association of Certified Fraud Examiners, the leading association in the prevention and fight against company fraud, has estimated that the already worrying levels of fraud will increase by 30 per cent in the short term as a direct consequence of the financial and economic crisis.[9]

4.3 OPPORTUNITY

The level of opportunity is directly and heavily influenced by the role that the individual plays within the organisation. The higher the individual is within the company hierarchy, the better he knows internal controls and the better he can elude them. In fact, the greater the power he has over the people who have to operate these controls and the easier

---

9   See Occupational Fraud: A Study of the Impact of an Economic Recession, Association of Certified Fraud Examiners, March 2009.

he can abuse his power to avoid these same controls. This straightforward observation explains the reason why, in reality, most unethical actions that turn out to be real fraud are committed by individuals who hold the highest positions within an organisation. According to a very recent study on a sample of 100 companies from different countries that were victims of fraudulent activities, in 11 cases the culprit was none other than the chief executive officer, whereas in 60 per cent of cases, fraud was perpetrated by senior managers or members of the board of directors. If middle management is included, the percentage of cases goes up to 86 per cent.[10] In monetary terms, other studies show that fraud committed by senior managers is, on average, 6 times larger than that perpetrated by management and 14 times larger than that committed by employees.[11] Moreover, statistics are corroborated by reality because in the Parmalat and Enron cases, just to mention the most sensationalised ones, all the top managers were corrupt, or at least, had colluded. It would be particularly difficult and, at any rate, illogical to commit a large-scale fraud without making sure that there is ample room for manoeuvre and good cover. Moreover, senior management involvement allowed, in both cases, the fraud to go on undetected for several years.

Since opportunity allows for the ease with which an individual can elude internal controls, there is no doubt that it is the one element, amongst the three making up the fraud triangle,

---

10   From Profile of a Fraudster – Survey 2007, carried out by KPMG, an international consultancy firm whose activities include the prevention of and fight against occupational fraud.

11   For further reading, please refer to the studies carried out by the Association of Certified Fraud Examiners (ACFE). ACFE is an association created in 1988 in the USA that has expanded into many other countries too. Its mission is to reduce the incidence of company fraud and to assist its members in their daily fraud prevention and detection activities.

that can be controlled most easily by the company and that requires particular attention from the individual responsible for ensuring the ethicality of company conduct. In fact, in order to minimise the risk of adopting unethical conduct, effective work needs to be done on corporate governance, i.e., the organisation's processes and the management and control systems exercised through legal and technical institutions and rules. Therefore, the company's organisational model needs to be carefully selected in order to, for instance, have the fundamental preventive internal controls to ensure adequate segregation of duties amongst individuals operating in a single process. In fact, an efficient system of internal controls provides for the various activities of a critical process to be carried out by different people. This way, individual employees who have to interact with other colleagues are unable to complete the process on their own. By acting in this way, mutual control among the participants in the process takes place spontaneously. This internal control will ensure that, for instance, the employee who logs suppliers' invoices cannot pay them, or that the person in charge of purchasing who creates the supplier master data does not issue purchase orders. In practice, it is a question of using an organisational model that does not delegate more power to individual people than their roles and responsibilities provide for. Obviously, if all the participants in the process were corrupt or colluding with each other, even this precaution would turn out to be useless. It is important to underline that, because all company transactions are now carried out using IT systems, the organisational structure based on the principle of segregation of duties has to be replicated to manage access to companies' IT systems and the rights of individual users.

A further example of a particularly effective preventive internal control is the adoption of procedures regulating in detail the way in which the company expects employees to behave in relation to a given process by limiting their "room for manoeuvre". If, for instance, a purchasing procedure specifies the types and amounts of expenses that employees can incur when travelling on business, an individual's discretion will be very limited and, consequently, it will be difficult to take advantage of special circumstances to the company's detriment. The creation of an Internal Audit Department, or the adoption of a whistle blowing procedure enabling everyone with genuine doubts on the moral propriety of actions taken by colleagues to report them, is an effective preventive control. The fact that anyone within the organisation can receive an unexpected visit from the auditors or can be reported to management because of questionable conduct contributes to keeping employees on their toes and, therefore, reduces the opportunities to adopt unethical behaviour.

4.4 RATIONALISATION

Rationalising means looking for motivations to justify one's unethical behaviour in an attempt to make it look more acceptable in one's own eyes and in other people's eyes if found out. The individual rationalises his actions in order to feel less guilty. If this were not so, he would not have the courage to act in this way. The classic rationale is: "I am not stealing. I am only taking what I am entitled to for all the sacrifices I have made in all the years I have been loyal to the company and which have never been adequately recognised." Rationalising is a very human attitude and, consequently, we take it on very easily and in different situations.

In the business world, rationalising is an attitude that turns out to be extremely dangerous because it leads to a sort of mental habit and creates unpleasant situations that are almost impossible to revert. In relation to this, Sherron Watkins, the executive of the Enron group who in 2001 reported the fraud said the following:

> *I think there are difficult moments of truth when leadership is tested. And if these moments are not faced honestly, if the hard decision is not made at that point, it becomes next to impossible to return to the right path. Once you start to rationalize, you're stuck.*[12]

Experts in company fraud, in particular, tell us that rationalisation is more common where there is lack of involvement and sharing on the part of staff in the company's activities. This automatically generates demotivation and frustration and, over time, can result in the conviction that the employer is being unfair. Management style, or the "tone at the top", therefore, becomes a crucial factor in monitoring employees' ability to rationalise unethical conduct. In particular, a strong authoritarian management style which does not provide for participation in company decisions by the various hierarchical levels is a clear risk. An analysis of the groups involved in the financial scandals of the beginning of this century has highlighted this aspect. These groups were all characterised by a decidedly authoritarian management style, if not dictatorial, and by a particularly charismatic character supported by close and very loyal aides. Taking into account the two emblematic cases of fraud of the beginning of the century, this dictatorial management style was typical of Jeffrey Skilling, Enron's CEO, and Calisto Tanzi, Parmalat founder and president. Adopting

---

12   From the interview with Sherron Watkins published in *The Fraud Magazine*, Jan/Feb 2007, the magazine of the Association of Certified Fraud Examiners.

an authoritarian management style creates a real gap between the "thinking mind" and the "operational mind" of the organisation. Thus, dangerous power and, therefore, control vacuums are created where fraud can easily take place. The adoption of a strongly participatory management style, through which top management takes on a clear stance vis-à-vis the fundamental nature of the ethical element within the company and its willingness to keep it in due consideration when carrying out daily activities, becomes a critical element to combat fraud. This important aspect will be dealt with later on in the discussion on company culture.

Another factor which strongly influences the level of rationalisation is the perception of the seriousness of the consequences if found out. The existence, seriousness and strictness with which repressive measures are applied play a critical role in the likelihood that unethical conduct becomes rationalised. To this end, Sherron Watkins, who had just been through the Enron experience, recalls that:

> *The major point I stress now is how and why company leaders must have a zero-tolerance policy for ethically challenged employees. It is probably the hardest role of a CEO, but when he or she discovers that an employee has violated the company's value system, that person must go.*

> *That's a tough one for most. Often we feel it's compassionate to forgive and forget and give them a second chance. And if the violator is a star, a superstar, who is great with the customers, or great generating revenues then you really want to forgive and forget.*

> *Trouble is that once you do that, you've sent the message throughout the organisation that the value system is second to being great with customers. Go ahead, push the edge of the envelope; if you get caught, you'll have a second chance.*[13]

As a matter of fact, for the risk of rationalisation to be mitigated, the control system must always provide for disciplinary and punitive measures to be applied to those who do not abide by internal rules, usually expressed as policies, ethical codes and procedures. It is obvious that, in the case of fraud, the civil and criminal codes will be the punitive system. However, for offences that cannot be prosecuted, internal policies and procedures providing for disciplinary measures should be used that are proportionate to the seriousness of the offence. They should even go as far as dismissing the employee.

Another typical way of thinking of someone who tries to rationalise the fact that he is about to commit fraud is to believe that "everybody does it" or that "it is normal". In some cultures, committing fraud in specific situations has become such a common practice – even amongst those who in other aspects of life usually adopt ethical behaviour – that public morals now seem to accept it. In Italy, for instance, tax evasion and tax avoidance are so common that the public does not seem to consider evaders as criminals. As pressure to comply with tax rules is no longer there, a vicious circle has been created whereby the number of evaders and the amount of money evaded have tended to increase with serious consequences for the country.

---

13   From the interview with Sherron Watkins published in *The Fraud Magazine*, Jan/Feb 2007, the magazine of the Association of Certified Fraud Examiners.

In 2008, for example, a study identified the total amount of income not reported to the fiscal authorities to be around 300 billion euros, on which Italians did not pay any taxes.[14]

4.5 TRADITIONAL RISK THEORY APPLIED TO ETHICAL RISK

The described fraud triangle theory explains the psychological dynamics that lead people to behave in one way rather than in another in relation to their sense of ethics. This is mainly due to a series of factors such as the fear of being caught or the psychological pressure people feel at some point to make money very quickly.

In this sense, it is extremely difficult to try to control these situations because they are the result of a combination of usually unpredictable factors. Even the fear of being found out, for instance, is highly subjective because it depends on the individual knowing the controls that the company has adopted and, at any rate, it depends on his own personal propensity to take risks.

While the need to implement risk assessment processes in the organisation to increase control over the risk will be discussed in Section 6.4, it is worth at this point to describe briefly the traditional risk management theory. This theory, in fact, tells us that there are four possible strategies to adopt in managing risk. They can be illustrated using the following risk matrix (Figure 4.1), where the impact of a given event arising from

---

14   "Evasione fiscale, 300 miliardi all'anno", *Corriere della Sera*, September 20th, 2008.

exposure to a given risk is plotted against the probability of that event actually occurring.

1. Retain: low-impact, low-probability risks are accepted or retained.

2. Mitigate: high-probability, low-impact risks are sought to be reduced.

3. Avoid: high-impact, high-probability risks should be avoided.

4. Transfer: high-impact, low-probability risks are transferred (e.g. insurance).

It is very difficult to apply these strategies to ethical risk given its previously outlined peculiarities. Nevertheless, for illustration purposes and in attempt to identify guidelines that can be useful to those within companies who have to assess and manage this risk, the following observations can be made.

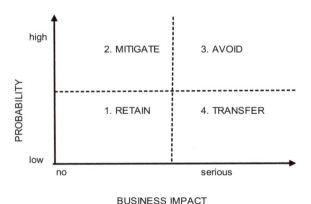

Figure 4.1   Risk matrix

RETAIN

One of the features of a lack of ethics is that before it is "discovered" it can go unnoticed for a long time. However, when it is brought to light and the public at large is informed about it, it can cause catastrophic damage. This feature makes prior acceptance of a lack of ethics a very dangerous and irrational choice and, as such, one to be avoided.

According to the most recent international studies, the average loss due to fraud amounts to 7 per cent of the value of each financial transaction (in the US alone, this figure translates to approximately \$994 billion in fraud losses[15]). It is natural to wonder who, in these days of global economic crisis, is prepared to accept these losses passively. Furthermore, studies carried out in this sector highlight that in environments characterised by moral laxity, cases of fraud increase much more rapidly because it is logical to expect this behaviour to be emulated if it is not repressed or punished at all.

For these reasons, the selection of a Retain risk strategy seems not to correspond to a sound management decision.

TRANSFER

Transfer of risk to third parties does not seem to be sensible or, at any rate, possible.

Transferring ethical risk to suppliers or business partners, i.e., transferring particularly delicate and fraud-prone processes, does not often offer any advantage. One example would

---

15   "2008 Report To The Nation On Occupational Fraud", Association Of Certified Fraud Examiners (ACFE), p. 8.

be currently common practice of outsourcing financial processes by transferring the accounting function to an external specialised company, or management of IT systems to an IT company. In reality ethical risk is not transferred but is increased because, if an accounting fraud were to be discovered, the company name (brand) would be jeopardised as if the fraud had taken place in house. What's more, if I externalise my processes, I tend to lose control over them and, in particular, of people managing them, thus increasing risk.

The only case in which a Transfer strategy can be useful is the instance that all the damages, including the collateral ones, related to the discovery of the unethical behaviour can be borne by, for example, an insurance company. Given how common fraud is and the huge sums of money to be paid out as compensation, I believe that even if insurance products of this type were available, their premiums would be prohibitively expensive for most companies.

MITIGATE

If risk is believed to be characterised by low business impact, then the strategy to pursue would be the Mitigate strategy. To mitigate ethical risk one would probably need to operate a number of detective controls. The purpose of detecting is to identify acts that have already been committed in an attempt to find the people who were responsible for them and take suitable measures against them. This type of control is particularly important as a deterrent for ill-intentioned employees who, by fearing that they are going to be found out, give up unethical conduct (reducing, as previously said, their capability to rationalise). A typical example of a detective measure to mitigate ethical risk is carrying out ethics or compliance audits.

If this path is chosen, then two elements need to be borne in mind:

1. International studies highlight how detective controls turn out to be little effective when unethical behaviour develops into fraud (almost half of the cases of fraud are, in fact, discovered following a tip or by accident).[16]

2. The intention to mitigate the risk could be an illusion because in reality it could show itself to its full extent when least expected and, at that point in time, there will be little chance to minimize the damage.

AVOID

If the objective is to eliminate (avoid) ethical risk, then the only real strategy that experience shows to be effective is that of prevention. This is the activity carried out beforehand to reduce the likelihood of an unethical event occurring. It is a question of ensuring that an individual faced with a moral dilemma voluntarily chooses the most desirable solution from an ethical point of view.

To attain this objective, the following measures are considered to be necessary.

1. Giving adequate consideration to candidates' moral values during recruitment;

2. Training staff to develop and strengthen their sense of ethics.

---

16   "2008 Report To The Nation On Occupational Fraud", Association Of Certified Fraud Examiners (ACFE), p. 18.

If, therefore, prevention can be considered the most effective strategy in ethics, it is also useful to highlight its difficulties and disadvantages:

1. It calls for considerable planning skills because, as the word itself suggests, it is a question of preventing a problem that could arise in the future and taking immediate measures to increase the likelihood that it will be resolved in an ethical manner in accordance with, for instance, the principles at the basis of the company's culture.

2. It calls for significant investment both in terms of staff dealing with the selection of candidates and the creation of performance evaluation processes that give adequate consideration to the ethical aspects, and in terms of lifelong training on ethical issues for every employee.

Taking into account practical financial implications, the solution most companies have adopted is a mix of prevention activities, such as the continuous provision of training to their staff, and detection activities, such as the creation of an internal audit department which carries out a number of yearly ethical audits.

The fact remains that if a company wishes to raise its ethical level even further because, for instance, it wants the general public to associate its brand with extremely ethical behaviour, it will have to invest more in preventative measures.

"The question before us is not whether the market is a force for good or ill. Its power to generate wealth and expand freedom is unmatched. But this crisis has reminded us that without a watchful eye the market can spin out of control. A nation cannot prosper long when it favours only the prosperous."

Barack Obama, US President, 20 January 2009

"A set of common principles and standards governing international economic and financial activity is an essential foundation for stable global growth."

From the Lecce Framework agreed by the G8 Finance Ministers, 29 June 2009

"To come out of the crisis, re-establishing spiritual and moral values that have been completely absent from decisions made by financial and economic entities and people is essential."

Giorgio Napolitano, President of the Italian Republic, 16 June 2009

"Rules in business are fundamental because they are also a tool bringing values, principles and ethics to the economic world."

Giulio Tremonti, Italian Finance Minister, 8 July 2009

"The question before us is not whether the market is a force for good or ill. Its power to generate wealth and expand freedom is unmatched. But this crisis has reminded us that without a watchful eye the market can spin out of control. A nation cannot prosper long when it favours only the prosperous."

Barack Obama, US President, 20 January 2009

"A set of common principles and standards governing international economic and financial activity is an essential foundation for stable global growth."

From the Lecce Framework agreed by the G8 Finance Ministers, 29 June 2009

"To come out of the crisis, re-establishing spiritual and moral values that have been completely absent from decisions made by financial and economic entities and people is essential."

Giorgio Napolitano, President of the Italian Republic, 16 June 2009

"Rules in business are fundamental because they are also a tool bringing values, principles and ethics to the economic world."

Giulio Tremonti, Italian Finance Minister, 8 July 2009

⑤ Areas on Which to Focus Efforts

5.1 EXTERNAL AND INTERNAL MEASURES

In relation to the tools that can be used to mitigate the risk of unethical actions, the following classification can be used: external measures – externally imposed onto individuals without them participating in their definition – and internal measures, with individuals actively participating in their definition. Let's analyse them in greater detail.

EXTERNAL MEASURES

Local, national or supranational laws and regulations, as well as specific organisation policies and procedures are all external measures. The advantages of this type of measure come from the fact that rules are formalised in writing, communicated through official channels and, therefore, most probably known by everyone who is asked to observe them. This leads to clarity when interpreting them as well as consistent behaviour, with all its subsequent advantages. The use of rules, in fact, makes it easy to identify a lack of compliance. Furthermore, applying repressive measures is feasible. Therefore, they play an important role in discouraging people who might be tempted to adopt unethical behaviour. In fact, because they perceive a real risk of being found out and facing disciplinary measures, they would find it hard to "rationalise" their behaviour and, most probably, would not adopt it.

There is a significant limitation ingrained in "external" remedies; laws and rules are often perceived as impositions and do not affect the nature and conscience of an individual. Consequently, individuals comply with the rules because they are forced to and rarely because they perceive them to be fair and necessary. In reality rules are adhered to only in proportion to the perception of the risk of being found out to be not in compliance with them and, eventually, sanctioned. If this risk is relatively low, or if the specific behaviour is not defined by a formal rule, then the individual will tend to "rationalise" unethical behaviour easily and, consequently, have no qualms about committing the crime.

INTERNAL MEASURES

Internal measures directly appeal to an individual's moral conscience which is linked closely to their personality and upbringing. These are measures that, unlike the external ones, are genuinely connected with the notion of ethics and are not dependent on the existence and application of laws and rules. (Incidentally, laws and rules might not even be inspired by ethical principles, an example being the anti-semitic laws of Nazi Germany or those on birth control in China.) The purpose is not to have a more ethical business world through the mushrooming of careful laws, but rather to promote and encourage the development of a moral conscience among individuals belonging to this world. By doing this, ethical principles will be applied on the basis of values that have been processed and interiorised by the individuals themselves and irrespective of the existence and content of any law.

The adoption of internal measures only would entail the lack of a frame of reference which individuals can turn to whenever they have to make ethically challenging decisions. In fact, ethical people end up making decisions that turn out to be ethically undesirable for the system as a whole because they are not fully aware of the consequences of their decisions or because they are not knowledgeable enough to judge them in a more general, and often complex, context. The recommendation is to adopt both internal and external measures simultaneously to achieve long-lasting results. Modern capitalism is betting on the realisation of the importance of this apparently trivial observation and on the efforts it needs to make to identify, for each type of measure, the initiatives that can lead to tangible results.

The following chapter will outline internal measures made popular by the school of thought which demands more ethical and responsible conduct from businesses and which has developed over the last few decades. No specific reference to external measures will be made because a discussion on laws and regulations is too technical for the purposes of this guide.

5.2 SPREADING A COMPANY CULTURE

Company culture encompasses all the unwritten rules, values, customs and styles which influence the expectations, thoughts and behaviour of people who operate within its organised structure. As such, a company culture is unique and cannot be replicated because it is a function of the people who work within the organisation. Its main components are the company's philosophy and management style.

COMPANY PHILOSOPHY

Over time, each organisation defines the values that meet with the approval of both top management and the rest of the employees and are shared and spontaneously applied by every member of staff. All these values make up the company philosophy. As it is the outcome of the interaction of the personalities of all members of the organisation, in defining them, management's charisma and leadership qualities play a fundamental role. Consider, for instance, how much these characteristics have influenced the development and definition of the company culture of what is now the most respected and admired consultancy firm in the world: McKinsey. In the 1930s, Marvin Bower, a young American lawyer, understood the enormous potential of what we now would call management consulting and began to work for McKinsey & Co, a small Chicago-based consultancy. In just a few years, he was able to transform the company into the best consultancy firm in the world and a true point of reference for the entire sector.

Bower believed that the philosophy and culture of a company had to develop naturally and almost through a trial-and-error process that improves over time. Every employee has to share these values, not because they are imposed but because they share their fairness and ethical basis and, consequently, they must be at ease when they apply them daily. In this sense, according to Bower, their formal definition through, for instance, a code of conduct, was unnecessary. The values expressed through the management's leadership and charisma were therefore conveyed to the rest of the organisation through a totally informal and natural process enabling them to be really absorbed and, consequently, practised. Obviously, for the process to yield the required results, it was fundamental to select the right people not only in terms of skills but also personality and moral values at every hierarchical level. McKinsey's company philosophy, as a set of values truly recognised and lived by all the employees, has become a point of reference for many other companies.

Bower attached great importance to the ethical aspect of the activities of the company he was managing and maintained that this was necessary to achieve the highest success for at least three reasons:

1. When there are well-defined ethical principles, people are more determined and efficient; there are no doubts and no time is wasted in considering possible alternatives;

2. A company practising recognised moral principles inevitably attracts high quality applicants, making the recruitment process much easier.

3. A company practising recognised moral principles establishes better and more solid relationships with its customers, competitors and the general public; everybody is aware that the company will do the right thing at the right time.[1]

---

1   From *The Will To Manage: Corporate Success Through Programmed Management*, Marvin Bower, McGraw-Hill, 1966.

MANAGEMENT STYLE

Over the last few years, in the field of internal audit and in other disciplines dealing with the ethical aspect of a company, the expression "tone at the top" has been coined to define the fundamental influence that top management has on the rest of the organisation. This influence strongly contributes to defining the company culture.

The management style of an organisation is determined by the following two components:

1. The degree of transparency of top managers' activities in relation to the company or Group shareholders.

2. The degree to which top management shares decisions with the different hierarchical levels. When there is real management sharing, top managers and all the other levels below them contribute to defining company policies and making decisions.[2]

According to the level and mix of these two components, management style fluctuates from participatory, when they are both present to the highest degree, to authoritarian.

A participatory management style, which attaches importance to communication between the various company levels, creates, under the same conditions, greater transparency and auditability of management's work both by management itself (a natural form of cross checks comes into being) and by independent functions, such as internal audit. This, therefore,

---

2   See *Frodi societarie e corporate governance* (Company Fraud and Corporate Governance), Chapter 3.5 "Area critica: stile di direzione" (A Critical Area: Management Style), Giorgio Lagana', Il Sole 24 Ore 2004.

will be the model of management style that an ethical company will want to adopt.

There are many types of negative behaviour that management adopts that exert a strong influence on the style which will characterise it in the eyes of the employees. The following are some of the more popular examples of this behaviour. Management:

- Communicates untrue results on company management to employees, shareholders and the public;

- Does not comply with accounting standards in order to pocket higher bonuses;

- Abuses company perks;

- Does not state a conflict of interest with the company;

- Does not comply with the code of ethics and company policies and procedures;

- Avoids internal controls for direct or indirect personal gain or to commit fraud;

- Does not take responsibility for decisions taken that are relevant to its sphere of competence;

- Uses company assets for personal purposes;

- Uses its position to control and manipulate employees;

- Uses working relationships (with suppliers, for instance) to obtain personal advantages.

Unless top management acts as a positive role model for employees, showing how to behave, the entire organisation will believe, at a subconscious level too, that the above behaviour is not important and that, therefore, everybody can adopt it. Experts in company fraud, for instance, highlight the fact that companies without an adequate tone at the top are more easily victims of fraud compared to those where management has adopted a style that is consistent with the moral values expressed by the company's code of ethics.

In reality, companies often convey conflicting messages to their employees: the company must act according to pre-set and formally communicated principles but management is the first to show that it does not believe in those principles and the way it acts is not consistent with them. As has already been seen, this message can be the outcome of the adoption of decidedly unethical conduct. The same undesirable result can be obtained by making decisions that are not necessarily unethical per se. In fact, by conveying a message inconsistent with the principles laid down in the code of ethics or, in any case, the best practice applied by most companies, this conduct is perceived by the employees as a serious lack of professionalism on the part of management and leads to a sudden loss of trust.

The following are some examples of the most frequent contradictions found in bodies that are responsible for ensuring ethics in a company: the internal audit and the compliance functions. Management:

- Does not create internal audit and compliance functions with clear responsibilities for identifying and pursuing breaches of ethical principles;

- Does not assign to these functions adequate decision-making powers to fulfil their responsibilities effectively;

- Does not ensure for them the necessary independence in terms of hierarchical lines;

- Does not adopt an accurate management information system when the problems highlighted by these two departments need to be urgently communicated and solved ("escalation process");

- Does not assign adequate resources to the compliance function to provide employees with the necessary training on the code of conduct.

5.3 THE EFFECTIVENESS OF CORPORATE GOVERNANCE MODELS

Opportunity within a company is also heavily influenced by its model of corporate governance. Even though several definitions of corporate governance have been formulated over time, a comprehensive one sees corporate governance as the structure through which the objectives of the company are set, and the means of attaining the objectives and monitoring performance are determined.

Once clarified what corporate governance is, it is pivotal to explain what good corporate governance means. The Financial Reporting Council, the UK's independent regulator, has set out the following definition in the Combined Code, i.e., the code of corporate governance:

> *Good corporate governance should contribute to better company performance by helping the board discharge its duties in the best interest of shareholders; if it is ignored, the consequence may well be vulnerability or poor performance. Good corporate governance should facilitate efficient, effective and entrepreneurial management so that can deliver shareholder value over the longer term.*[3]

The following are examples of conditions that a good corporate governance model must meet:

- The creation of management and control committees and bodies, and establishment of a system of regular meetings to ensure efficient and effective management through sharing high-level information and a transparent decision-making process;

- The assignment of specific responsibilities to the different company roles and the definition of clear reporting lines;

- The creation of independent bodies to control company management and compliance with laws;

- The adoption of rules preventing conflicts of interest;

- The implementation of an efficient internal control system; and

---

3   The Financial Reporting Council (FRC), the Combined Code, June 2008.

- The impartial selection of the external auditing company to be responsible for the certification of the balance sheet;

- In the case of a Group, its legal structure should be consistent with its business activities and should not be artificially complicated by creating, for instance, several holdings.

Since a company's circumstances vary over time, its corporate governance model has to evolve in line with this and must be reviewed continuously for it to remain effective. This implies that there is no single standard model but there must be processes to oversee its suitability over time in relation to, for instance, any regulations that define its requirements, functions and effectiveness.

The concept of corporate governance is rather complex in that it includes a series of components and aspects which, from time to time, take on different importance in creating an "opportunity", as defined in fraud theory and, therefore, turn out to be more or less risky. The following is a short illustration of what are usually considered to be the main components of the corporate governance of an organisation.

MISSION, VISION AND STRATEGY

The mission defined by every organisation identifies the fundamental purpose at the very basis of its creation. In practice, it summarises in a sentence the organisation's *raison d'être*. In the case of a car company, for instance, its mission could be: "To create cars for which our customers perceive an added value". Rather than the mission, some organisations prefer to define the main values with which the company identifies and which inspire its choices and priorities. British Petroleum, for instance, one of the largest oil and energy companies, in its value statement states that:

> *BP wants to be recognised as a great company – competitively successful and a force for progress. We have a fundamental belief that we can make a difference in the world. We help the world meet its growing need for heat, light and mobility. We strive to do that by producing energy that is affordable, secure and doesn't damage the environment.*[4]

Like its mission, every organisation defines, more or less formally, its vision, that is to say the future, projected and desired state of the organisation in terms of its long-term objectives and strategic direction. In the case of a car manufacturer, an example of its vision could be: "To become one of the three market leaders in the manufacture and distribution of medium sized cars" or "To become the leading car company in the production of low pollution engines".

The company strategy is a plan defining the allocation of human and financial resources to achieve the objectives of the company. The strategy is a fundamental document to manage the company itself and ensure that objectives are actually achieved.

Vision, mission and strategy are three fundamental components of corporate governance, since they define the nature and purpose of the organisation and dictate the direction that the company must follow during its development and consolidation. In this sense, they are essential elements to

---

4   From British Petroleum's Value Statement, www.bp.com.

assess the ethical aspect of an organisation. For example, the definition of the nature of the activities performed by a company is fundamental to understand the ethics inherent in its business. Those who believe that arms production is unethical would probably not invest in or do business with a company whose vision is "to become the largest manufacturer of fighter jets and missile systems". They would also hesitate to deal with a company whose description of its activities in its vision is not in line with its actual activities. Even though it stated that it was an energy company, in the 1990s, i.e., at the height of its fraudulent activities, Enron, the American energy giant, was acting as if it were a financial company becoming involved in risky financial trading operations and paying bribes to politicians in various countries.

ORGANISATION CHART

The basic document used to define responsibilities and hierarchical lines within a company is its organisation chart. It is used to understand who manages the company, what the operational and support departments are, and the way in which each of them relates to the others in terms of reporting lines. An organisation chart is usually visually represented to enable an immediate understanding of the company structure. Its analysis shows if the type of company structure is strongly hierarchical or more participatory. If the former has been chosen, the chart will be markedly pyramidal, with few departments at the bottom but many hierarchical levels. In the second scenario, the reverse will be true and the chart will be more horizontal. As previously mentioned, a participatory management style is reflected in a rather "flat" structure and, because it means greater involvement in company decisions by the various hierarchical levels, it facilitates the adoption of more ethical conduct.

JOB DESCRIPTIONS

A job description is a document describing the role played by each individual within a company, his hierarchical position within his department and his reporting lines.

In terms of reporting lines, if the organisation chart highlights the relationships between the various company functions and the committees that have to manage the organisation, a job description is a document defining in greater detail who the individual employee reports to within the function to which he belongs.

With regard to decision-making powers, as established by the hierarchical position, qualifications and responsibilities, the job description has a dual purpose:

1. Assigning decision-making powers to individuals who have the necessary competences to exercise them;

2. Assigning accountability in relation to the decision-making powers.

The organisation chart, together with the job descriptions, describes the entire company's structure. When drawing them up, special attention needs to be paid to the following aspects:

1. They have to be clear and transparent so that everyone knows their own duties and responsibilities as well as those of other individuals and bodies contributing to the management of the company;

2. They have to be communicated and shared, i.e., everyone must be aware of and accept them;

3. They should not have any "gaps", i.e., areas of responsibility not assigned to specific functions and/or individuals;

4. They should be balanced, i.e., they should avoid situations for which a decision-making power is not matched by a responsibility and vice versa.

Balancing powers and responsibilities is a fundamental aspect because it ensures that whoever had to make a decision actually took it; if this were not the case, he would have to justify this. Similarly, anyone who has made a decision will no longer be able to shirk his responsibility. The more confused the power/responsibility relationship, the more the excuses presented by people who should have not only managed effectively the company, but also ensure its ethical conduct.

COMMITTEES

Many company decisions, particularly those of a strategic nature, are made by committees, i.e., a group of individuals who, after studying the details of a problem, vote in order to take a joint decision on it.

As in the case of individual employees, the problem relating to the balance between decision-making power and responsibility holds true for committees as well. In this case, the committee's competences and all the rules governing its operation should be formally defined in a document: the Charter. The Charter will include the following: name of the committee, areas of responsibility, chairman and secretary, members, frequency of meetings, how decisions are made and relationships with any other committee.

A fundamental aspect to ascertain the proper operation of a committee is to check that the subjects it deals with and on which it makes decisions are written down in the minutes of its meetings and that these minutes are promptly circulated to the members for their comments and approval. The minutes will have to be drawn up as if they were an action plan in order to solve the problems that have been discussed. They will have to be updated at the following meeting by including the progress made on previously discussed matters. A similar system ensures that all the issues a committee is responsible for and that are raised by the various departments and employees are discussed during the committee meetings and effectively solved over time.

SUPERVISORY AND MONITORING BODIES

A further fundamental component of corporate governance is the bodies in charge of monitoring and supervising company management. The ones that are most concerned with ethics within the company are the Audit Committee (and the auditing department that usually reports to this Committee) and the Compliance and Ethics department. Both are described in greater detail in the next chapter.

INTERNAL CONTROL SYSTEM

Internal controls are structures, activities, processes and systems to help management mitigate the risks of not attaining company objectives. In this sense, a system of internal controls is also pivotal in supporting management in complying with their company's ethical standards generally expressed in a code of conduct approved by the Board. Internal controls, for example, help in identifying cases of non-compliance with laws, regulations and policies or detecting cases of fraud.

RISK MANAGEMENT

Risk management is a process aiming at identifying all company risks and, therefore, it involves an entire organisation. In establishing such a process, management want to identify the risks that could prevent the company from achieving its objectives. Their identification, in fact, enables management to adopt action plans to mitigate the likelihood of risks arising or, at any rate, their business impact.

Nowadays, large organisations create specific functions whose responsibility is to implement risk management processes and monitor risk levels over time. One of the outcomes of risk management is ethical risk (see Chapter 6, Section 6.4: Risk Management Function).

5.4 THE STUDY OF ETHICS

The study of ethics is one of the issues in the field of ethics on which economists and scholars have expressed rather contrasting opinions over the centuries. The 2004 article by John Hooker, Professor of Ethics and Social Responsibility at the Carnegie Mellon University in the USA entitled "The Case Against Ethics Education: A Study in Bad Arguments"[5] is a summary of arguments against the study of ethics. In this article he refutes the validity of these arguments one by one.

---

5   "The Case Against Ethics Education: A Study in Bad Arguments", an article by John Hooker, *Journal of Business Ethics Education*, 2004.

1. "The task of managers who run companies is to maximise profits for shareholders". This is called the Milton Friedman argument because he was the first one to suggest it. In practice, he maintained that the only objective of those who manage a company on behalf of shareholders is that of maximising profits. Managers, therefore, are neither qualified nor entitled to implement social policies unless they are a means to maximise company profits. Hooker specifies that managers are not asked to implement social policies but to deal with the impact that their organisation has on civil society and the environment. In relation to being entitled to do so or not, Hooker presents a simile. As in the case of a company directly run by its owner, who takes on the social responsibilities inherent in the business of the company, similarly, if the owner were to entrust the management of his company to an agent, this would logically have to fulfil the same social responsibilities. Stating the opposite would be like saying that a mafia man is not responsible for the murder committed by his henchman.

2. "Ethics in itself is not an incentive to apply it; financial (gains) or legal incentives (savings from avoiding fines or penalties) are needed". Hooker points out that incentives are necessary but not sufficient to create an ethical system. Thinking that the economic system can base its own ethics just on incentives is utopian because it is tantamount to saying that it is sufficient to pass a law for this to be automatically observed by everyone. The reality is quite different because, for instance, there are no adequate mechanisms to verify compliance with the law and few monitoring and law enforcement bodies which, sometimes, are even corrupt.

3. "Ethics is an innate quality of an individual that does not entail intellectual activity and is the not the result of reasoning". Consequently, it cannot be learnt. Hooker responds to this argument by pointing out how, in the course of history, the greatest "intellectuals" have discussed ethics and contributed to its development. He also recommends attending a class in ethics to realise what it means to deal with ethics in practice by, for instance, analysing real moral dilemmas.

4. "Ethics is learned by the individual only as an adolescent and, therefore, by the time he goes to university, it is too late to learn it". Hooker points out that, even though an individual's personality can be shaped already when he goes to university, the study of ethics aims at changing behaviour rather than personality. In this sense, learning the conceptual infrastructure on which to base one's thinking, learning the various advanced theories over time, analysing how real ethical dilemmas have been dealt with and resolved, distinguishing between the various possible ways of thinking and avoiding mistakes that are usually made, help individuals to think in terms of ethics. Hooker adds another particularly important motivation. Referring to the most recent developments in the field of psychology, he questions the fact that only during adolescence is personality fully formed. Various studies show that the evolution of personality goes through various stages, some of which occur during adulthood. In this sense, the study of ethics could also have an important influence on personality as well as on behaviour.

5. "There is no motivational incentive to learn ethics and, therefore, teaching it is useless". Many students are not really interested in courses on ethics because, in their

opinion, there is no reason to do so as it will not help further their career. Some teachers try to get round this lack of motivation by teaching the vision where profits can be maximised through ethics too. This is quite a popular vision and it is one that often leads companies to launch and finance humanitarian projects of various natures. However, the rationale at the basis of these projects can hardly be considered ethical because it is purely based on financial returns. Hooker moves away from this notion and, starting from the assumption that we are all interested in doing some "good", tries to convince his students that one's own social responsibilities can also be fulfilled by making profit.

5.5 SELECTING, ATTRACTING AND RETAINING "ETHICAL" STAFF

Selecting those people who, from a moral point of view, are more valid will be increasingly important in the future for two reasons:

1. To lower company exposure to risks, such as fraud and reputational risks;

2. To create a working environment that attracts and retains individuals who are more in tune with the ethical culture of the company.

STAFF SELECTION THAT IS MORE FOCUSED ON THE ETHICAL ASPECT

At the base of economic transactions there are values, such as trust in the other party, which are recognised in every country to varying degrees. These values are reflected not only in the laws and regulations of individual countries but also in international or supranational laws and regulations. Usually, those who do not comply with them do not have access to the world of work. In fact, it is common practice, at the beginning of a career, to undertake a selection process where an individual who, for instance, has committed certain types of crimes is not accepted (at least not by the official world of work). Candidates are invariably requested to submit documents such as criminal records and references from previous employers when applying for jobs. Furthermore, respect for these principles has to be proven not only when the individual is first hired but also when he changes employers. Given the high level of flexibility in the modern world of work, this could in fact happen several times during one's career.

Therefore, working on the rules followed for selecting whoever enters the business world, particularly those who are chosen for positions carrying particular responsibilities within it, would seem a logical and necessary step to increase the ethical level in the business world. Current staff selection procedures ought to concentrate more on understanding a candidate's ethical measure, particularly their ability to distinguish morally acceptable conduct from conduct that is not, as well as their propensity to make decisions consistent with this criterion of discernment. It is now common practice to use questionnaires and interviews to assess the character and psychology of applicants whereas very little is still done to assess their ethicality. As early as the 1940s, Marvin Bower, founder of McKinsey, the most admired consultancy firm in the world, was attaching great importance to the selection of his staff, which aimed at assessing not only their technical skills but also the level of adherence to the moral principles at the very basis of McKinsey's philosophy.

Over the last few years, many researchers and experts have suggested that candidate intelligence ought to be evaluated on the basis of criteria that are different from Quantitative Intelligence (IQ), i.e., the intelligence enabling us to make rapid abstract links typical of mathematics.[6] In the 1990s Daniel Goleman, in particular, expounded the theory of emotional intelligence, based on those skills that in short enable an individual to relate to others and convince them to cooperate with him. More recently, the theory of emotional intelligence has been further developed giving rise to moral intelligence. In their book entitled Moral Intelligence – Enhancing Business Performance and Leadership Success,[7] Doug Lennick and Fred Kiel describe the outcome of their large-scale research work during which they interviewed a high number of chief executive officers in large companies to understand the distinguishing features that have led them to excel in the world of work. In particular, this is how they arrived at identifying moral intelligence as soon as they finished with their investigation:

> As we talked, we realized that we had some common ideas about the ingredients of high performance that we were both struggling to conceptualize. We agreed on the importance of emotional intelligence, the constellation of self-awareness, self-management, social awareness, and relationship management skills that are now commonly regarded as critical to success in the workplace (they were all highlighted by Daniel

---

6   Further reading: *Social Intelligence: the New Science of Success* by Karl Albrecht, *Emotional Intelligence, Why It Can Matter More Than IQ* by Daniel Goleman, and *Frames of Mind: the Theory of Multiple Intelligences* by Howard Gardner.

7   *Moral Intelligence – Enhancing Business Performance and Leadership Success* by Doug Lennick and Fred Kiel, Wharton School Publishing, 2008 edition.

Goleman's work). We discovered, though, that neither of us thought emotional intelligence was sufficient to assure consistent, long-term performance... We hypothesized that there was something more basic than emotional intelligence skills, a kind of moral compass, that seemed to us to be at the heart of long-lasting business success. We decided to label this "something more" moral intelligence.

Subsequently, they defined moral intelligence as the "mental ability to establish how universal moral principles must be applied to our values, objectives and actions". In other words, it is the capacity to differentiate between "right" and "wrong" according to universal ethical principles, that is to say, those relating to human behaviour and common to every culture.

ATTRACTING AND MAINTAINING MORALLY VALID HUMAN RESOURCES

According to what the experts tell us, over the next few years, the main criteria for understanding candidates will be their alignment to the vision, objectives and culture of the company, aspects referring to the ethical element of the organisation.[8] Therefore, selecting people with an adequate ethical profile according to what has just been described is fundamental for creating a working environment that is perceived as ethical by future employees. Ultimately, companies that want to succeed will have to apply selection criteria focusing more on values and ethicality to ensure they hire personnel who stand out from a moral point of view too. In doing so, they create a suitable working environment to attract new resources with

---

8   "The War of Talent" published in *The McKinsey Quarterly*, No. 3, 1998.

a high ethical profile. This virtuous circle will ensure a strong company culture and highly motivated staff. In the long term, this process will generate a more robust organisation, able to adapt to change better and react to difficulties more quickly.

5.6 FAIRNESS OF INCENTIVE SYSTEMS

One of the few positive effects of the financial crisis of 2008 is that it brought to light the risk of inadequate incentive systems. In fact, for years in the banking sector, there has been an exponential growth in the remuneration of "bankers", i.e., those executives and top managers working for investment or commercial banks. Usually, their remuneration is made up of a salary and a bonus. The second part of their remuneration is often extremely high and greatly exceeds that of similar professionals working in non-financial sectors.

In the autumn of 2008, following the beginning of the financial crisis, George Osborne, the British MP who was shadow Chancellor of the Exchequer, called for a change to bankers' pay stating that "*The party is over for the banks. You can't go on paying yourselves 20 times what a heart surgeon earns!*".[9]

The problem with incentives is that they are often linked to short-term profits rather than long-term ones. This fact pushes individuals to take on investments and business with risk profiles higher than the ones they would have normally considered reasonable. This leads to an illogical situation in which a professional earns enormous sums of money even when the company he works for has incurred losses or, as was the case for some companies during the financial crisis

---

9   From "Treasury's Bank Bonus Team to Get Own Payout", an article published in *The Times* on 9 February 2009.

of 2008, has been nationalised to avoid bankruptcy because it was considered "too large to fail".

Recent events within the context of the financial crisis have further highlighted that this system entails three risks:

1. It is socially destabilising because the inequality that it creates between the various social and professional classes leads to worrying social tension.

2. It is economically destabilising because by promoting a short-term vision it makes the entire economic system unstable and puts it at constant risk of collapsing.

3. It is ethically destabilising because if the system collapses, those who pay for the consequences of this are taxpayers most of whom are not responsible for managing the system.

In October 2008, the Securities & Investment Institute (SII), the professional body for thousands of people who work in the securities and investment industry in the UK, issued a real policy to define fair and transparent bonuses. The purpose of this policy is to encourage its members and the general public to acknowledge the need to change the parameters that have been used so far to calculate bonuses in the financial sector.[10]

The following are the core principles outlined in this document:

---

10   The Bonus Policy issued by the Securities & Investment Institute in October 2008 can be downloaded from the Institute's website: www.sii.org. uk/web5/infopool.nsf/HTML/mIntegrityPosition-Paper.

1. Recognition and support of the concept of paying people an element of remuneration in recognition of achievements in their employment that are over and above what would normally be expected.

2. These achievements may not always result in additional income accruing to the firm because they could translate into greater savings or prevention of losses.

3. A bonus should take into account not only the contribution of an individual but also that of their team/division and the overall performance of the firm/company.

4. A bonus should also take into account factors other than profit, such as co-operation with others, compliance with procedures and training of others.

5. A bonus should reflect factors such as the risk that the company has taken on in doing a deal and the quantity of the firm's capital used. The amount of the bonus will be inversely proportional to these two parameters.

6. Payment of a bonus should not be front loaded and should be spread over a period relevant to the transaction e.g., between two and five years. This is to allow time for the results of the underlying transactions upon which the award was made to be properly evaluated.

7. Bonus awards should be indicative to allow the possibility of clawing back part or all of the bonus award should it emerge at a later stage that the underlying transaction was not as profitable as first thought. Similarly, the reverse could apply.

8. In the case of a quoted company, the higher the bonus award, the greater the proportion which should be paid in shares. This ensures that the objectives of the individual are aligned with the shareholders and encourages a long-term approach.

9. The larger an award compared with an employee's basic salary, the greater the need for it to be signed off by an independent body within the firm, such as the Remuneration Committee.

10. The annual accounts of firms should, in future, provide a level of disclosure above the statutory minimum on bonus payments. This way, transparency would increase.

In light of these considerations, bonuses, as an incentive system adopted by the financial sector, must be reviewed in order to have a greater degree of fairness within the general scheme of remuneration. Fortunately, some countries seem to have understood this lesson and have introduced some changes and have taken operational measures to solve this problem. International bodies such as the Financial Stability Forum (which, during the G20 summit held in London in April 2009, became the Financial Stability Board), which brings together Finance and Economic Ministers and central bankers of some of the countries belonging to the G20, and the European Commission, has recently set some guidelines that banks have to follow when defining remuneration systems for their employees. It has also introduced in its agenda further discussions on this issue to lay down more specific rules, in an attempt to create greater transparency in the remuneration of bankers and the results of the financial institutions they lead. The real challenge, however, lies in the harmonisation of these new rules because their effectiveness will be greater or lower according to the measures that other countries will adopt and implement. In fact, it is logical to assume that, if there are wide differences between what a banker can earn in one country as opposed to another, many of them will leave the country to move to more lucrative shores.

(6) Company Functions Responsible for Monitoring and Overseeing Ethics

6.1 AUDIT COMMITTEE

In 1939, the New York Stock Exchange was the first to define the concept of an Audit Committee, i.e., an operational committee made up of a number of Board members responsible for selecting external auditors and periodically communicating with them to keep abreast of any administrative and accounting problems. The importance of this committee has increased enormously and, in order to ensure its transparency and effectiveness, its composition has evolved too. In 1972, the Security Exchange Commission stipulated that only non-executive board members could join Audit Committees of listed companies. In 1977, the New York Stock Exchange required that the Audit Committees of all listed companies be made up of independent advisor members. In practice, there are two conditions with which members of Audit Committees usually have to comply:

1. The non-executive nature of the members: advisors are not members of management; as such they are not employees and play no operational role within their organisations;

2. Independence: members should not find themselves in circumstances, which, according to the Board of Directors, can invalidate their ability to evaluate and judge objectively. In general, members are not considered independent in those situations where they might be acting out of private interests or, at any rate, not fully in line with company interests. For instance, they cannot own company shares nor can they be related to any member of Management nor have any professional relationship with the company, including supplying products or services.

The Sarbanes and Oxley Act, a US law passed in 2002 following the financial scandals of the beginning of the millennium, has significantly increased the responsibilities of Audit Committees. Its provisions have been followed by the Stock Exchange Commission which in 2003 introduced a series of requirements, such as the independence of Audit Committee members, to be followed by all companies listed in the American markets, including those controlled by foreign groups.

Although Audit Committees are currently responsible for a whole series of activities – from selecting external auditors to supervising financial and accounting processes – the responsibilities that are more closely related to ethics are as follows:

1. Overseeing compliance with laws and regulations, and ethics in general, including the whistleblowing procedure;

2. Overseeing the activities of the Internal Audit department;

3. Verifying the implementation of risk management processes and discussing with Management the outcome of these activities.

This chapter will analyse how the need for overseeing compliance with laws and regulations has led to the creation of a real company function, the Ethics and Compliance department, with responsibilities for the issues that have just been discussed. The need to adopt a whistleblowing procedure will be dealt with later on together with tools that can assist to increase ethics in companies. This chapter will also review the organisation and responsibilities of an internal audit department as well as the need to have effective risk management processes.

6.2 THE ETHICS AND COMPLIANCE DEPARTMENT

In 1991, the USA introduced the Federal Sentencing Guidelines for Organisations, a set of rules for financial frauds, sexual harassment and dangerous products. These rules apply to every type of company, including unlisted ones, but do not impose any obligation. Nevertheless, the incentive to comply with them is strong because, should any type of fraud or illegal act be uncovered, the judge will take compliance to the

Guidelines into account when sentencing and may decide to significantly reduce the sentence provided for by law.

In 1992, a document entitled *Internal Control – Integrated Framework* was published by the Committee of Sponsoring Organisations of the Treadway Commission (COSO). COSO is a private sector US initiative dedicated to identifying factors that enable the disclosure of fraudulent and fabricated financial statements and issuing suggestions to limit their extent. Commonly known as the COSO Report, it outlines a methodology that organisations can follow to assess and improve their internal controls. There are five integrated components within this methodology, one of which is the "control environment" that sets the tone of an organization, influencing the control consciousness of its people. It is the foundation for all other components of internal control, providing discipline and structure. Control environment factors include the integrity, ethical values, management's operating style, delegation of authority systems, as well as the processes for managing and developing people in the organization. The model emphasises the significance of having a specific "ethical" function within the organisation so that the "control environment" is as favourable as possible to facilitating ethical behaviour by its employees and by the company as a whole.

In answer to both the Federal Sentencing Guidelines for Organisations and the COSO Report, from the beginning of the 1990s the large American corporations, followed by the corporations of the other modern economies, started to create Ethics and Compliance departments to comply with the guidelines. Since then, the number of organisations with specific Ethics and Compliance departments has increased rapidly. This trend received a further boost in 2002 in the aftermath of the Enron financial scandal, when the Bush Administration passed the Sarbanes and Oxley Act. Some sections of this law, in fact, are very specific about the duties and tools that organisations listed in the US markets must have in terms of ethics and compliance.

In summary, the mission of an Ethics and Compliance department is as follows:

- To ensure that the organisation complies with the highest levels of integrity and ethics;

- To ensure compliance with laws and regulations which are relevant to the company's business; and, more generally,

- To create a culture characterised by honesty and integrity and aimed at promoting efforts to "do the right thing" in any circumstance.

Every organisation of a certain size now has an ethics and compliance function, usually made up of members from the Legal department. In some cases, though, the Human Resources department can be involved given its natural function to provide guidelines to staff and answer their queries.

As the Audit Committee is responsible for ensuring that the organisation abides by laws and regulations and that its work can be considered ethical, the Ethics and Compliance department usually reports to the Audit Committee, as does the Internal Audit department. In the absence of an Audit Committee, the ethics and compliance function will report directly to the Board of Directors.

In the case of supranational organisations, there will be a contact for ethics and compliance in each local unit reporting to someone in charge of ethics at group level. This person is often a member of the Ethics and Compliance Committee which supervises the overall activity of this function from an operational point of view and ensures that it works effectively and that, for instance, all problems are duly solved. This Committee is normally made up of the person responsible for ethics at group level, the group legal counsel and some members of senior management. It is usually the person in charge of ethics and compliance at Group level, i.e., the global compliance officer, who periodically reports to the Audit Committee on the activities carried out and the main problems that have been encountered.

The main duties of the Ethics and Compliance department can be summarised as follows:

- Assessing and identifying risks related to its sphere of competence through consultations with the Ethics and Compliance Committee and all the other departments in the organisation;

- Defining and issuing policies and procedures aimed at ensuring compliance with rules and ethical conduct; these include the code of conduct;

- Training and guidance, in conjunction with other departments, on policies and procedures and, more generally, risk areas;

- Implementing and managing tools and procedures to report violations anonymously, i.e., the whistleblowing procedure (or Compliance Helpline);

- Creating opportunities to ask for information and clarify doubts;

- Support the business in writing policies and procedures and reviewing processes, activities, risk areas and other related issues;

- Verifying the adoption of disciplinary actions in the case of violation of laws, and policies and procedures in conjunction with Human Resources;

- Responding promptly and effectively to problems and requests related to compliance with rules and ethics.

6.3 INTERNAL AUDIT DEPARTMENT

Immediately after the Second World War, larger companies began to set up Internal Audit departments solely responsible for ensuring that the accounts were accurate. Over the last few years, the responsibilities of Internal Audit departments have significantly changed and expanded. Following the ratification of the Sarbanes and Oxley Act in 2002, the visibility of internal audit has expanded considerably because it was recognised as one of the most important tools in the prevention and fight against occupational fraud. In 2004, the New York Stock Exchange made it compulsory for listed companies to have an internal audit department that could provide management and the Audit Committee with systematic evaluations of the effectiveness of risk assessment processes and internal control systems. Similarly, a large number of Stock Exchanges in other parts of the world have adopted rules that, in special circumstances, have made the creation of internal audit departments compulsory. Unlisted companies do not usually have to comply with this requirement. Nonetheless, most businesses above a certain size voluntarily decide to have an internal audit function because it is now considered good practice to ensure effective control over company management.

To gain a better understanding of the fundamental function of internal audit, the notion of "internal controls" needs to be clarified. Considering that management responsibility is to mitigate the risk of not attaining company objectives, "internal controls" are structures, activities, processes and systems to help management fulfil this responsibility. The Board of Directors ensures that management fulfils this responsibility. A structured, independent and effective internal audit department assists both management and the Board of Directors, by reporting to the Audit Committee, in fulfilling their responsibilities. By using a systematic and disciplined audit approach, it provides an objective opinion on the effectiveness of internal controls and risk management processes.

The Institute of Internal Auditors, the sector's international professional association, has formulated the following definition of contemporary internal audit:

> *Internal audit is an independent, objective assurance and consulting activity designed to add value and improve an organisation's operations. It helps an organisation accomplish its objectives by bringing a systematic, disciplined approach to evaluate and improve the effectiveness of risk management, control, and governance processes.*[1]

---

1   2006 version of the official definition of internal audit as supplied by the Institute of Internal Auditors (IIA).

In summary, the main responsibilities of internal audit are:

1. Ensuring that the organisation achieves its operational and strategic objectives;

2. Ensuring that the company's operational activities are performed efficiently and effectively;

3. Ensuring compliance with all relevant laws and regulations as well as internally developed policies and procedures;

4. Ensuring the truthfulness and accuracy of operational and financial information;

5. Ensuring that there are suitable controls in place to safeguard all company assets;

6. Ensuring that an effective system of internal controls is in place;

7. Ensuring that systematic risk assessments are carried out.

The independence requirement of internal audit greatly depends on the reporting lines of the department in relation to the rest of the organisation, while the objectivity requirement depends on the frame of mind of the Chief Audit Executive (CAE), i.e., the head of internal audit, and the department staff. These two fundamental requirements will be analysed in the following pages.

The independence of internal audit is better ensured by the following reporting lines. They describe what has now become best practice because internationally adopted by most companies. According to this model, the head of the internal audit department reports to two bodies simultaneously: management and the Supervisory Committee:

1. From an administrative point of view, the CAE reports to management because internal audit is an integral part of the organisation and needs to receive adequate support for daily internal audit activities. In this sense, the CAE and management interact on issues such as budgeting and human resources, internal information, and administrative activities related to, for instance, the approval of travelling expenses and paid leave.

2. The Supervisory Committee is usually the Audit Committee or, in its absence, the Board of Directors. In summary, the interaction between the Supervisory Committee and the audit department refers to:

   - Approving its charter, including mission, objectives and strategy;
   - Approving budget and staffing level;
   - Approving the yearly auditing plan;
   - Holding regular meetings during which the CAE reports on auditing activities and their outcome; the CAE can also call meetings to discuss important facts and can ask that management does not take part in these meetings;
   - Approving the CAE's appointment, dismissal, promotion and remuneration;
   - Setting any limit in terms of actions or financial resources if they are considered to be insufficient to fulfil responsibilities.

In the past, the CAE reported to the chief financial officer or the CEO and internal audit was considered, therefore, more an activity carried out *for* management (which, as a result, tended to control it) than for the Board of Directors and shareholders. In recent years, however, the CAE's independence from management has increased with the above-mentioned changes in hierarchical lines. Therefore, another important auditing activity *by* management *for* the Board of Directors now ranks alongside the auditing activity *for* management. Its purpose is to protect shareholders' interests more tangibly. The dual hierarchical line for the CAE ensures that, if there are serious problems within the company, management cannot unduly influence the auditing plan, the scope of auditing activities or the way in which the outcome of these activities are communicated to senior managers. Compared to the past, internal audit is now an activity carried out more for the benefit of the Board and, ultimately, the shareholders.

The objectivity of the Internal Audit department is ensured by the fact that its staff, in preparing judgements and evaluations, always take all relevant circumstances into due account without being influenced by their own interests or those of others. Therefore, conflicts of interest with the objectives of the department or the company are averted.

In ethical terms, internal audit is helpful in a number of instances:

1. Audits to verify that the entire organisation abides by external laws and regulations;

2. Audits to verify the ethics of company policies and procedures, including the whistleblowing procedure;

3. Audits to verify compliance with the code of ethics;

4. Audits to verify compliance with internal policies and procedures;

5. Audits of the Ethics and Compliance department to verify its structure and the functioning of its processes;

6. Audits of the risk management processes that should include the ethical risk;

7. Fraud investigations.

It is clear that, when it comes to ethics, the role of internal audit is quite vast. This is mainly due to the following:

1. Internal audit is an independent function and this ensures that its work is objective;

2. The department's charter, approved by the Board of Directors, gives auditors plenty of room to manoeuvre in terms of selecting audits to carry out as well as documents and information to review;

3. Internal auditors have a deep knowledge of the external as well as their companies' regulatory environment;

4. The selection process and the qualifications required from internal auditors ensure their high professionalism which is constantly kept updated through continuous training on fundamental subjects related to their profession such as ethics.

6.4 RISK MANAGEMENT FUNCTION

Risk management is a process aiming at identifying all company risks, evaluating the company exposure to these risks and implementing adequate mitigation processes.

In recent years, the importance of risk management has grown significantly and now, following the 2008 financial crisis, it has been recognised as a fundamental component of an effective corporate governance model.

Section 404 of the 2002 US Sarbanes-Oxley Act requires that companies listed in the US markets use a well-defined control methodology when auditing internal controls. As a result, many companies have chosen to apply the COSO Internal Control Framework issued in 1992 by the Committee of Sponsoring Organizations (COSO), which includes risk assessment as a prerequisite for determining how the risks should be managed. Subsequently, other regulations, such as those of the Security Exchange Commission, have requested that greater attention be paid to top-down risk identification and assessment, i.e., cascaded down from top management to lower levels of management. Hence, in the last decade the majority of companies have implemented some form of risk assessment tools and processes to help them to implement the traditional risk management strategy described in Chapter 4, Section 4.5, that identifies four approaches to risk: Accept, Mitigate, Avoid and Transfer.

In 2003, the New York Stock Exchange specified that the Audit Committees of its listed companies must discuss with top managers policies and procedures on risk assessment and management. While CEOs and senior management are responsible for assessing and managing their companies' risk exposure, Audit Committees discuss the guidelines governing the processes. In particular, they discuss financial risks and the measures that management should undertake to mitigate its effects.[2]

In order to deal with these regulations and, in particular, to strengthen company governance, a high number of companies over the last few years have established a Risk Management function responsible for implementing risk management processes and monitoring risk levels.

When risk analysis concerns the entire organisation and risk management processes are embedded in all company processes, this becomes a more comprehensive and sophisticated approach to risk and is called Enterprise Risk Management.[3]

Every employee contributes to risk management. However, management has the primary responsibility for implementing it in a structured, consistent and coordinated way. As has already been stated, the Audit Committee is responsible for ensuring that risks are monitored and managed at an acceptable level. In fulfilling its responsibility, the Audit Committee can direct internal audit activity to assist him by examining, evaluating, reporting, and recommending improvements to the adequacy and effectiveness of management's risk processes.[4]

Ethical risk is one of the outcomes of risk management and, therefore, this process should be established by all companies

2   From the NYSE Listing Standards, Part 7d.

3   See "Enterprise Risk Management_Integrated Framework" by Committee Of Sponsoring Organisations of the Treadway Commission (COSO), September 2004.

4   See IIA Position Paper "The Role of Internal Audit in Entreprise-wide Risk Management", September 2004.

wishing to improve their ethical levels. Even though it depends on the definition that each company uses for ethical risk, the following risks can be included in this category:

1. Compliance risk: i.e., failure to abide by laws and regulations adopted by nations or other supranational bodies as well as internal company policies and procedures. This latter category includes risks associated with failure to comply with the company's Code of Ethics, the internal document defining ethical rules and principles that the organisation, starting from its own Management, recognises and complies with in carrying out its daily business.

2. Fraud risk: this includes not just so-called occupational fraud, i.e., fraud committed by employees, but also fraud committed by organisations to the detriment of third parties in an attempt to obtain special terms illegally.

3. Reputational risk: this is the risk that the company image is associated with a negative, or perceived as such, event. If, for any reason, public opinion does not recognise the company as a socially responsible entity because, for instance, it is harming the communities in which it operates or because its industrial production pollutes the environment, it can launch disparaging campaigns against the company.

6.5 STRENGTHENING "ETHICAL" FUNCTIONS

All the latest international regulations underline the importance of strengthening a company's ethical component by demanding that company functions be created with specific ethical aims and by trying to equip them with the most suitable tools to achieve their objectives. The ongoing financial crisis that started in 2008 is only the latest event to remind us of the risk of jeopardising the sustainability of the economic system in the long run when the ethical side of business is neglected. It is therefore desirable that governments and institutions make more effort to introduce higher levels of ethics. One of the effects of these efforts will be the strengthening of company functions responsible for this aspect: the Ethics and Compliance and Internal Audit departments and the Risk Management function.

In the case of the Ethics and Compliance department, the main trends aimed at strengthening visibility, effectiveness and available resources are as follows:

1. Enhancing training activities for everyone, from new employees to top managers and members of the Board of Directors;

2. Greater financial resources and more skilled human resources;

3. Greater authority to the head of the Ethics and Compliance department;

4. Greater focus on development and monitoring of the code of conduct;

5. More attention paid to effective implementation of the whistleblowing procedure and its alignment to specific company and cultural circumstances.

Developments in ethics could have a greater impact on the internal audit function which, compared to the ethics and compliance function, has had a longer and more troubled history, born as it was almost a century ago. In particular, the main foreseeable trends aimed at strengthening the activities of internal audit, so that it can have a more effective impact on the ethical aspect of companies, are as follows:

1. Making the creation of an internal audit function mandatory for companies listed in all financial markets and/or of a certain size. The Combined Code on Corporate Governance (the reference code on corporate governance for English businesses) recommends, e.g., the creation of this function but does not state that it is compulsory.

2. The CAE's status and level of competence ought to be on a par with that of an executive director; in general, this means increasing his authority and visibility within the company but also his accountability if, for instance, he fails to inform the Board of Directors of negative events that he should have foreseen and prevented.

3. Increasing the number of meetings between the CAE and the Audit Committee and strengthening the way they communicate.

4. Greater involvement in risk management. Internal audit is expected to perform all activities necessary to align company risk to the level that the Board of Directors believes to be acceptable (risk appetite).

5. Assisting the Audit Committee in strengthening its activities around understanding and enhancing the organisation's governance processes, moving governance from form to substance.

A significant part of the business world seems to agree on the fact that one of the most important lessons of the 2008 financial crisis is that the banking system, but similarly any other industry, needs to re-think the design and implementation of its risk management processes. This fact highlights the necessity of having a dedicated function within the company that manages these processes.

The current main trends of the Risk Management function are as follows:

1. Increasing funding and human resources assigned to this function.

2. Transitioning from identification of tactical risks to more strategic ones.

3. More participative and collaborative forms of risk identification and evaluation: "workshops" are used to brainstorm and discuss risk.

4. Appointing a Chief Risk Officer (CRO), the executive responsible for enabling the efficient and effective governance of risk, and related opportunities.

5. Establishing a risk committee to coordinate the activities of the risk function.

6. More effective monitoring of risk to verify effectiveness of mitigation actions.

7. Use of scenario analysis to identify emerging risks and evaluate their business impact.

8. Difficulty in creating a centralized risk management plan, where risk information is consolidated.

(7) Tools to Make Companies More Ethical

7.1 THE CODE OF CONDUCT

Each organisation has its own philosophy that reflects the values communicated by its management and is displayed through its conduct and management style. This philosophy is, or should be, known to all members of the organisation and be put into practice by them at any time. For this to happen, it is fundamental that the organisation formalises these values through an official document called the Code of Conduct. This is an essential step in order to have higher ethical standards within the organisation.

Even though large US corporations had already adopted the first codes of conduct in the 1960s, it was only at the beginning of this millennium that their adoption became a widespread practice. In 2007, the International Federation of Accountants defined the Code of Conduct as follows:

Principles, values, standards, or rules of behavior that guide the decisions, procedures and systems of an organization in a way that:

(a) contributes to the welfare of its key stakeholders; and

(b) respects the rights of all constituents affected by its operations.[1]

The content of a code of conduct is based on the following main principles:

- Compliance with laws and regulations;

- Condemnation of every form of sexual harassment and discrimination in the workplace;

- Adoption of behaviour characterised by transparency and the avoidance of any type of conflict of interest;

- Commitment not to adopt any anti-competitive practices;

- Commitment to protect company information and assets;

- Support of and contribution to the development of the communities where the organisation operates;

- Commitment to preserve and protect the natural environment.

---

1   The International Federation of Accountants, www.ifac.org.

According to the activities performed by the organisation, other more specific principles can obviously be included such as, for example, the commitment not to employ child labour if the company has operations in developing countries.

A code of conduct entails different and significant advantages for the company adopting it, including:

1. Increased Employee Motivation and Enthusiasm

   Recent studies have indicated that 94 per cent of employees believe company ethics to be a fundamental aspect of their working lives; 82 per cent of them would even be prepared to sacrifice part of their salaries and work for a company with ethical business practices if they were reassured that the company works according to acceptable ethical levels.[2]

2. Strong Tone at the Top

   The fact that top management officially releases a code of conduct and states that it intends to abide by it in any circumstance is a strong incentive for the entire organisation to embrace the values expressed by the code and put them into practice. This is a strong message for both employees and the general public.

3. Better Company Reputation and Business Relationships

   In the eyes of the public, companies are responsible for the moral conduct of their partners, customers and

---

2   From "Ethics Study: The Effect of Ethics on Ability to Attract, Retain, and Engage Employees", research carried out by the consulting company LRN, June 2006.

suppliers. As it is common practice to ask these parties to abide by their own codes of conduct, companies adopting such codes spread a culture based on ethics, thus bettering their reputation in the eyes of the public. For customers, suppliers and partners, there will also be greater incentive to expand their relationships with the organisation in question.

The Ethics and Compliance department is responsible for ensuring that the company adopts a suitable code of conduct and that the staff complies with it. In particular, the department deals with the following issues:

- Definition: ensuring that the content of the code is complete and accurate; specific company circumstances, linked to factors such as how international the business is, local cultures and customs, specific sectors of activity, impact on the environment and local communities.

- Adoption: in order to have an adequate tone at the top, it is fundamental that the code of conduct is agreed and approved by senior management;

- Communication: the code will undoubtedly not be observed unless all the employees are aware of it and have their own copy.

- Training: usually, the content of the code is not always immediately understood by every employee; training sessions, perhaps with case studies, are quite important to help employees to understand its content and, ultimately, to absorb its values.

- Compliance: this is the aspect that definitely requires greater effort because it is a lasting commitment; the Ethics and Compliance department usually facilitates this activity by adopting a reporting system for all cases of violation of the code.

- Disciplinary actions: in case of breach, the Ethics and Compliance department, in conjunction with Human Resources, ensures that adequate disciplinary sanctions are imposed; this is a fundamental aspect to convey to the organisation the clear message that management is determined to enforce the values expressed by the code in any circumstance.

Overall, the monitoring activities performed by the Ethics and Compliance department are solely based on staff and third parties (such as customers, suppliers and former employees) reporting genuine or alleged breaches or just expressing their worries about compliance issues. In this sense, the activity of the department can be considered "passive" because the process must be initiated by others. If, however, the organisation adopts a code of conduct, the internal audit department will be able to perform "active" monitoring of the ethical dimension by carrying out audits to verify compliance with the code itself.

Although a code of conduct is an excellent tool, its efficacy and the way it impacts on real conduct by the organisation and its people depends on various factors, such as the example set by top management, the training provided and the sanctions in case of failure to comply. Writing a code is not sufficient to ensure that staff automatically adheres to it. Enron, the American energy giant, had adopted a 64-page code of ethics when the financial fraud that caused its collapse was uncovered. Well before 2001, the notorious CEO of the company, Kenneth L. Lay, had distributed the code to all employees along with an introductory letter whose final paragraph stated: "We want to be proud of Enron and to know that it enjoys a reputation for fairness and honesty and that it is respected."[3]

Over the last few years, a tendency to define and adopt sectorial codes of conduct has developed. These codes are agreed with companies belonging to the same business sector that decide to adopt it across the border. This strategy is particularly important in sectors of social interest, such as the pharmaceutical and medical sectors, where it is fundamental that the values adopted are proper and exhaustive, and observed by the entire sector. The tendency to adopt sectorial codes of conduct has recently spread to other sectors. This is a positive factor because, by standardising conduct in businesses operating in the same sectors, transparency towards potential clients increases and public confidence can be increased too.

7.2 ADOPTING A WHISTLEBLOWING PROCEDURE

Whistleblowing is a company procedure enabling anyone – including employees and third parties such as customers and suppliers – to report anonymously illegal conduct or situations that they believe to be in breach of:

- National or supranational laws and regulations;

---

3   From the introductory letter to Enron's Code of Conduct, www.thesmokinggun.com.

- Company policies or procedures;

- Sectorial or company codes of conduct.

In the 1970s, some large organisations made the first attempts to implement the whistleblowing procedure. Initially, it was adopted mainly by companies that had dealings with civil servants in order to report cases of public corruption. When the fraud committed by Enron, the energy giant, came to light in 2001 thanks to Sherron Watkins, one of the group's vice-presidents, the use of this procedure to report wrongful conduct within businesses received greater attention. The Sarbanes and Oxley Act, passed in 2002 in the USA immediately after this financial scandal, strengthens a particularly delicate aspect of this procedure: protection of the "whistleblower", i.e., the person reporting the breach. The law, in fact, bans any company, employee, supplier or agent from dismissing, suspending, harassing, demotivating or discriminating against the person who has reported an alleged violation or contributed to an investigation.[4] In the UK, the Public Interest Disclosure Act 1998 provides for legal protection of the whistleblower.

The following sections describe the main characteristics for implementing an effective whistleblowing procedure.

CLEAR COMMUNICATION

In order to ensure that this procedure encourages staff to report alleged violations, it is important to formulate it in such a way as to reflect company culture as much as possible. Its wording has to be straightforward and clear. If the message is weak or unclear, staff will not be willing to come forward and report

---

4   See Section 806, Sarbanes and Oxley Act (2002).

the breach. The following points need to be borne in mind when drawing up the whistleblowing procedure:

1. Clear definition of cases of violation covered by the procedure;

2. Names of individuals the whistleblower needs to communicate with; leaving some choice to the whistleblower is good practice;

3. Ensuring anonymity and protection of the person reporting the breach and, until the investigation is over, the person under investigation;

4. Ensuring that the individual who will have to evaluate the outcome of the investigation does not take part in it;

5. Complete description of the various phases of the investigation;

6. Informing staff that, in specific circumstances, they have the legal right to report to individuals who do not belong to the organisation and specifying these circumstances.

VIOLATIONS COVERED BY THE PROCEDURE AND CIRCUMSTANCES REQUIRING INTERVENTION

- A criminal act has been or is about to be committed;

- An individual has violated or is about to violate a law he or she is supposed to comply with;

- A miscarriage of justice has taken place or is about to take place;

- The health and safety of an individual is or is about to be at risk;

- The environment has been or is about to be damaged;

- Information on the above circumstances has been or is about to be deliberately eliminated.

WHISTLEBLOWER'S GOOD FAITH

To ensure that this procedure is effective, the whistleblower's good faith is fundamental. Usually, the good faith requirement is met when the whistleblower:

- Believes in all honesty that this information is substantially true;

- Does not act out of revenge, jealousy or the like;

- Is not looking for personal gain.

ANONYMITY AND CONFIDENTIALITY

Even though a whistleblower usually receives legal protection against any form of retaliation, he or she is also entitled to report the fact anonymously. This right is available in order to provide a psychological incentive to those who find themselves in the position of having to report significant breaches in which, for instance, the company's top managers are involved.

In order to ensure that this procedure is effective, the identity of the whistleblower remains confidential even though it is known to the person who has officially taken the report. If it turns out that the people under investigation have to be informed of the whistleblower's identity, the latter's prior permission has to be obtained.

ESCALATION

As the breach that needs to be reported can involve the very people in charge of initiating the reporting and investigating procedures, the whistleblower usually has the possibility of liaising with a department immediately above the one usually responsible for initially dealing with reports.

PHASES OF THE PROCESS

The person formally receiving the report has to:

1. Inform the whistleblower of receipt of the report and, if the reported violation is regulated by the disciplinary procedures issued by Human Resources, the need to follow them;

2. Prepare an investigation plan that will include names of the investigation team members, names of the people to be interviewed, documents to be reviewed, timing of the various activities, how the outcome of the investigation will be documented and who the outcome will be communicated to.

DISCIPLINARY ACTIONS

As has already been stated, in relation to compliance with the code of conduct, it is important to take disciplinary action towards those who have failed to comply with the rules. Therefore, even in the case of violations brought to light through the whistleblowing procedure, the Ethics and Compliance department is responsible for ensuring that adequate corrective measures are taken vis-à-vis the offenders. Corrective actions will depend on a number of factors, including, for instance:

- Significance of the violation in terms of consequences for the organisation;

- Whether clear responsibility has been identified;

- Whether the violation has been made voluntarily:

- Whether the violation has legal consequences because there has been a breach of the law;

- Any mitigating circumstances.

BENEFITS

A whistleblowing procedure, if carefully adopted, offers huge benefits to the organisation:

1. It increases trust on the part of customers and the general public;

2. It can act as an early warning system of the ethical and compliance levels within the organisation because staff is often aware of undesirable conduct or violations;

3. It increases mutual trust among staff because it will support a culture based on honesty and transparency;

4. If the procedure is not adopted, there is a risk that the violation that would have been reported takes place causing greater harm;

5. It ensures that the great majority of irregularities are uncovered.

On this last point, the Association of Certified Fraud Examiners, the leading organisation in the fight against and prevention of occupational fraud, states that fraud identified thanks to reports received by whistleblowers amounts to 46 per cent of all cases. This fact makes this the most effective tool for identifying illegal activities in companies.[5]

---

5   See the "2008 Report To The Nation", by the Association of Certified Fraud Examiners (ACFE), p. 18.

On the effectiveness of different tools to uncover fraud, it is interesting to note that:

a)   The adoption of a whistleblowing procedure in 2008 concerns 46 per cent of cases but only 34 per cent of cases in 2006 (the survey is bi-annual), It is likely that the greater use of this procedure among companies and its better adaptation make it not only the most effective tool but also the one that leads to better improvements over time.

b)   Casuality, internal controls and internal audit – all three at the relatively stable level of 20 per cent of cases – follow whistleblowing;

c)   The remaining tools are external auditing (around 10 per cent of cases) and notification from the police forces (around 4 per cent of cases).

7.3 ETHICAL OR COMPLIANCE PROGRAMMES

An Ethical or compliance programme provides a formal framework for ensuring that the business as a whole, as well as individual employees and directors, complies with laws, regulations and company policies and procedures.

Compliance programmes are an important part of the Federal Sentencing Guidelines for Organisations and the COSO Report that have been previously described. Both these sources emphasise how important it is for an organisation to have programmes ensuring that procedures are systematically followed.

The main benefits of the implementation of a compliance programme are as follows:

- Prevention of ethical misconduct;

- Avoidance of reputational damages;

- Avoidance of monetary losses incurred to pay fines;

- Enabling the organisation to adapt more quickly to sudden changes (regulatory changes, new technologies, mergers and acquisitions, etc.);

- Facilitating relations with stakeholders;

- Informing suppliers about the company's own standards.

The principal components of a compliance programme are:

1. Code of conduct;

2. Ethics training for personnel;

3. Reporting mechanism (i.e., the wistleblowing procedure);

4. Audit system;

5. Investigation system.

Since each organisation has its own culture and characteristics, not every programme will contain all the components but a combination of them, and the emphasis on each will vary.

For the programmes to be as effective as possible, it is important that before drawing them up, some analysis is carried out. The first thing to do is to identify the organisation's ethical characteristics by:

1. Finding out how board members, shareholders, Management, employees and other members of the organisation define "success";

2. Establishing if ethics is a success factor for the organisation;

3. Establishing if company values have been properly communicated and whether they are known;

4. Verifying if the company has written policies and procedures to regulate ethical aspects;

5. Understanding why staff would commit unethical acts;

For a compliance programme to be considered "effective", it has to include all the following aspects:

1. Promotion of specific principles and procedures that every employee has to comply with to achieve a reasonable reduction in the likelihood that they commit criminal acts;

2. Investing in people who are responsible at management level for monitoring compliance with these principles and procedures (i.e., Chief Ethics Officer, Chief Audit Executive);

3. Communicating principles and procedures effectively – also through specific initiatives – by asking that people take part in training programmes and by distributing literature explaining what is required in practical terms; Launching specific initiatives to verify compliance to principles and procedures using monitoring and auditing systems specifically developed to identify criminal acts, and introducing a reporting system for these acts;

4. Applying principles and procedures systematically on pain of disciplinary action; such action also needs to be taken against those who should have identified the criminal conduct;

5. Once a crime has been discovered, undertaking all necessary activities to adequately respond to it and prevent similar crimes in the future.

7.4 SUPPORT FROM PROFESSIONAL ASSOCIATIONS

There are two main factors at the basis of the increasing attention paid to ethics in companies and that have made ethics a priority in the Board's agenda:

1. The increasing levels of fraud in companies. Compared to 2008, levels of occupational fraud increased by 76% in 2009, resulting in 2 billion pounds going missing in the UK alone.[6]

2. The lack of adequate ethical levels make the economic system unstable and in danger of collapsing as shown by the 2008 financial crisis.

Having described the systems and professionals a company can use to procure higher ethical levels, as well as the tools that can be adopted, there is one aspect worth mentioning because it can be particularly useful in pursuing this objective. Over the last few years, a high number of international organisations and associations have been set up. Their mission is to support companies in introducing greater ethics and transparency. In general, they have the following objectives:

1. Suggesting best practices to companies, specifically in the fields of ethics, compliance, internal audit and fraud;

2. Making available documents, books, research and publications on the subjects of their specialisation;

---

6   According to the study on occupational fraud by accounting and consulting firm BDO LLP, January 2010.

3. Creating a network among practitioners to increase communication and facilitate knowledge sharing.

Given the high number of these organisations and associations and because their importance depends also on their presence in individual countries, it is particularly difficult to identify the most significant ones. The following section attempts to give some indication to anyone looking for information and advice on the various areas of ethics from organisations specialising in those areas. The list is ordered by relevant field and by geographic predominant presence.

ETHICS AND COMPLIANCE

International
- LRN: www.lrn.com

- Ethisphere: http://ethisphere.com/

UK
- Institute of Business Ethics: www.ibe.org.uk

- The Ethical Corporation Institute: www.ethical corporationinstitute.com/

- Centre for Business and Public Sector Ethics: www. ethicscentre.org

USA
- Ethics Resource Center: www.ethics.org

- Centre for ethics and business: www.ethicsandbusiness. org

- Society of Corporate Compliance and Ethics: www. corporatecompliance.org

- The Ethics and Compliance Officer Association: www. theecoa.org

AUDIT AND INTERNAL AUDIT

International
- Institute of Internal Auditors: www.theiia.org

UK
- The Institute of Chartered Accountants of England and Wales: www.icaew.com

- Association of Chartered Certified Accountants: www. acca.co.uk

USA
- American Institute of Certified Public Accountants: www. aicpa.org

- International Auditing and Assurance Standards Board: www.ifac.org/IAASB/

FRAUD/CORRUPTION

International

- Transparency International: www.transparency.org

- Association of Certified Fraud Examiners: www.acfe.org

UK

- The Fraud Advisory Panel: www.fraudadvisorypanel.org

- Serious Fraud Office: www.sfo.gov.uk

USA

- National White Collar Crime Center: www.nw3c.org/

RISK MANAGEMENT

International

- Institute of Risk Management (IRM): www.theirm.org
- Committee of Sponsoring Organizations of the Treadway Commission: www.coso.org
- Global Association of Risk Professionals (GARP): http://www.garp.com/

MULTI-AREA

The following are the largest international audit networks that cover all the above-mentioned areas, normally by having established specialised divisions within their organisation:

- PricewaterhouseCoopers: www.pwc.com

- Ernst & Young: www.ey.com

- KPMG: www.kpmg.com

- Deloitte: www.deloitte.com

⑧ Conclusions

Even though ethical uncertainty has always characterised the business world, its negative effects are today perceived more consciously. People have started to identify them and assess their impact with greater clarity. Reputational damage, loss of clients and sales, international disrepute, boycott campaigns, penalties, and loss of talented human resources are only some examples of the immediate consequences of conduct that the public considers to be unethical. When ethical uncertainty becomes a conscious decision not to comply with laws and regulations, it becomes a real crime and transforms itself into corruption when, for example, it is aimed at winning business illegally, or in occupational fraud when it is at the expense of employers. The latter type of fraud can show itself in its various guises, from conflict of interest to embezzlement, from cybercrime to false accounting. The economic and financial consequences of the ongoing and evolving crisis that started in autumn 2008 should highlight the need to adopt new rules but, above all, to spread a more solid culture based on respect for recognised ethical principles. Only education founded on these principles and the spreading of a culture based on them will enable and, to a certain extent ensure, future rules passed by governments and regulatory bodies will actually be complied with.

Adequate education and role models will enable adolescents to grow in an ethically sound environment and, therefore, to learn to adopt morally correct conduct even when this entails difficulties and sacrifices. The process of learning ethics must then carry on over the years, because future businessmen within modern capitalism must get used to facing with the right tools those moral dilemmas they will inevitably come up against in performing their tasks and fulfilling their responsibilities. They will be asked to solve these dilemmas not only in the interests of the company they will be representing, but also in the interests of all those who interact with the company and are affected by its decisions and conduct. Particular attention will therefore have to be paid to issues such as the environment and the protection and development of the communities in which companies operate. Universities and business schools need to teach ethics as a fundamental and integral part of the knowledge that is necessary in order to access the business world and be successful in it. There ought to be some form of "verification" of whether ethics has been learnt at the time when graduates enter the world of work. This could be done through tests and interviews and any time an individual is taking on a position of responsibility because of the significance of the impact that his decisions could have on the economic and social system in general.

The commitment that will hopefully be widespread in the corporate world will involve, in particular, the creation of Audit Committees on the agenda of which ethics will be one of the main priorities. In facing and solving these problems, the Audit Committee will be supported by an Internal Audit, an Ethics and Compliance department and a Risk Management function according to the specific competences and responsibilities of each of them. It is important to ensure that there is an adequate "tone at the top", i.e., management's willingness to put informally communicated principles into practice by creating a sound company culture and, in a more formal way, by adopting a code of conduct. Management style too will have an important effect on the entire organisation in terms of its ethicality: it is desirable for it to be as close to a participatory style as possible, thus allowing every hierarchical level to take part in the decision-making process and in the development of company policies. Regular training activities play a fundamental role in trying to raise the ethical level of an organisation. Particular attention ought to be paid to this activity and adequate resources ought to be assigned to it.

In future, those company functions that are also responsible for overseeing ethics and, if necessary, raising its level will play an even more important role. It is therefore necessary that Boards of Directors give these functions the necessary powers and resources to fulfil their responsibilities. The process of creating and strengthening "ethical" functions within companies started only a few years ago, but following the recent economic and financial crisis it is desirable that this commitment will deepen even further. Issues related to corporate governance, risk management, compliance with laws, ethics audits, anonymous reporting of misconduct, prevention and identification of fraud will have an increasing weight in the post-crisis business world. Over the last few years, international associations, institutes and bodies specialising in these issues have been created. Their research and analysis activities are excellent sources of information for professionals working in this field. Moreover, new professional figures have developed in the field of company ethics, such as the Ethics and Compliance Officer and the Chief Risk Officer. Often, they are accredited by internationally recognised professional associations to provide effective support to companies in their efforts to increase ethical levels.

In the post-crisis years, companies will no longer have excuses to avoid organising themselves effectively so that the way they operate is ethical both in terms of complying with laws and regulations and in the eyes of the public. An ethical company will enjoy an unprecedented competitive advantage and this will have a two-fold positive effect. At the level of the economic system, by acting in this way the risk that formed the basis of the current crisis will be limited and, therefore, similar crises will be averted in the future. At the level of the social system, greater alignment of company objectives with social objectives will create a host of advantages, which will ultimately translate into a better quality of life for everyone.

If you have found this book useful you may be interested in other titles from Gower

A Short Guide to Operational Risk
David Tattam
Paperback: 978-0-566-09183-4

A Short Guide to Political Risk
Robert McKellar
Paperback: 978-0-566-09160-5
e-book: 978-0-566-09161-2

A Short Guide to Procurement Risk
Richard Russill
Paperback: 978-0-566-09218-3
e-book: 978-0-566-09219-0

A Short Guide to Reputation Risk
Garry Honey
Paperback: 978-0-566-08995-4
e-book: 978-0-566-08996-1

Visit **www.gowerpublishing.com** and

- search the entire catalogue of Gower books in print
- order titles online at 10% discount
- take advantage of special offers
- sign up for our monthly e-mail update service
- download free sample chapters from all recent titles
- download or order our catalogue